A Crash Course on

Affiliate Marketing

A Comprehensive Beginner's Guide to Building Massive Passive

Income by Leveraging the Most Lucrative Niches

William R. Quick

Legal Disclaimer

The information provided in this book is for general informational purposes only. While every effort has been made to ensure the accuracy and completeness of the information presented, William R. Quick makes no representations or warranties of any kind, express or implied, about the completeness, accuracy, reliability, suitability, or availability with respect to the information, products, services, or related graphics contained in this book for any purpose. Any reliance you place on such information is strictly at your own risk.

In no event will William R. Quick be liable for any loss or damage including without limitation, indirect or consequential loss or damage, or any loss or damage whatsoever arising from loss of data or profits arising out of, or in connection with, the use of this book.

By reading this book, you agree to the terms and conditions outlined in this legal notice.

Request for a Review

Dear Valued Reader,

I hope you enjoy **"A Crash Course in Affiliate Marketing: A Comprehensive Beginner's Guide to Building Massive Passive Income by Leveraging the Most Lucrative Niches"** and find the information both useful and informative. Your input is vital to me, and I would be grateful if you could share your ideas by posting a review.

Your review not only aids in the discovery of the book by other aspiring affiliate marketers, but it also gives vital insights into your own experience. If you feel the book merits five stars, your recommendation may have a big influence.

Please visit https://amazon.com and share your opinions to post a review. Your candid opinion will help shape the future of this book and guide others on their affiliate marketing journey.

Furthermore, I invite you to contact me if you have any questions, recommendations, or difficulties while exploring the affiliate marketing topics in the book. Your success and comprehension are my top concerns, and I'm here to help.

Please feel free to contact me personally at williamquick92@gmail.com I'm here to assist if you have a question regarding a particular idea or need clarity on an approach.

Thank you for taking the time to read this and consider expressing your opinions. Your help meant everything to me.

Best Regards,

William R. Quick

williamquick92@gmail.com,

Gain Access to More Books by Me

Table of Contents

Introduction

Once upon a time, in a busy metropolis, a young and ambitious man called Alex lived. Alex was attracted by the immense prospects offered by the internet world, particularly the exciting field of affiliate marketing. Alex found himself at the crossroads of curiosity and ambition, intrigued yet uncertain where to begin.

Alex's enthusiasm with the notion of producing passive income by leveraging other people's goods kindled the first flame. Breaking away from the usual 9-to-5 grind and delving into the realm of internet business was both exciting and intimidating.

The sheer number of material became a labyrinth as Alex ventured further into the realm of affiliate marketing lessons and blogs. Chiang Mai, Bangkok, and Berlin, locations often listed as digital nomad hotspots, appeared planets distant from Alex's present position. The goal of working from anywhere in the globe seemed a long way off.

At this critical juncture, Alex came upon a book called **"A Crash Course on Affiliate Marketing: A Comprehensive Beginner's Guide to Building Massive Passive Income by Leveraging** *the **Most Lucrative Niches.*** The title was a perfect fit for Alex's path - a crash course to fast-track success in the difficult world of affiliate marketing.*

The author provided a vivid image of what was to come in the book's introduction. Alex's dedication was motivated by the promises of complete insights, the roadmap for novices, and the alluring potential of creating massive passive income.

The shroud of doubt started to dissipate as Alex engaged himself in the Introduction. The book evolved from a guide to a mentor, providing a road map for turning ambitions into real accomplishments. Alex quickly flicked the page, eager to absorb the knowledge that would chart the road for his affiliate marketing experience. Alex had no idea that this crash course would be the impetus for a voyage beyond his wildest dreams.

Brief Overview of Affiliate Marketing

Affiliate marketing is the technique by which an affiliate gets a commission for promoting the goods of another individual or business. The affiliate simply finds a product they like, promotes it, and receives a percentage of the proceeds from each transaction. Affiliate links from one website to another are used to monitor sales.

It is often regarded as an important component of current digital marketing. Affiliate marketing is appealing to organizations because it allows them to achieve their marketing objectives at a minimal cost. It helps affiliates by providing them with the possibility to earn passive income.

Affiliate marketing helps affiliates by providing them with the possibility to earn passive income

Creating an affiliate income demands the creation of a platform and the growth of an online audience. Affiliate marketing has grown in popularity as a result of the internet. Amazon popularized the practice by establishing an affiliate marketing program in which websites and bloggers place links to the Amazon page for a reviewed or discussed product in order to get advertising revenue if a purchase is made.

Affiliate marketing is, in this sense, a pay-for-performance marketing scheme in which the act of selling is outsourced over a large network. Affiliate marketing predates the Internet, but in the age of digital marketing, analytics and cookies have transformed it into a multibillion-dollar business. A company that runs an affiliate marketing program may analyze the links that bring in leads and see how many convert to sales using internal statistics.

An affiliate may help an e-commerce company access a larger audience of internet users and consumers. An affiliate may possess many websites or email marketing lists; the more websites or email lists an affiliate has, the larger its network. The recruited affiliates then communicates and promotes the e-commerce platform's products to their network.

Recruited affiliates communicates and promotes the e-commerce platform's products to their network.

This is accomplished by the affiliate via running banner advertisements, text ads, publishing links on its websites, or sending emails to clients. Advertisements in the form of articles, videos, and pictures are used by businesses to attract the attention of an audience to a service or product. Visitors who click on the advertisements or links are sent to the e-commerce site.

If customers buy the goods or service, the e-commerce merchant funds the affiliate's account with the agreed-upon commission, which may range from 5% to 10% of the transaction price.

Importance of Building Passive Income

Passive income enables you to generate money while doing other activities. Rental property, investments, and dividends from shares are examples of passive income sources, as are affiliate marketing, providing courses based on areas of specialized knowledge and skill, and publishing books. So basically, affiliate income, is the commission generated when a user purchases anything after clicking on a link on a website.

The importance of building a passive income includes the following:

a.   Passive income allows you to have more spare time.

Many people see time as one of the most important things since, unlike money, it cannot be earned again. Time is a limited commodity. Passive income allows you to spend your time doing activities you like rather than activities that are necessary to pay the bills.

This does not indicate that you are free of all life responsibilities; rather, it implies that you have the flexibility that comes with not having to fight to make ends meet at the end of the month. You are free to spend your time as you choose as long as your passive income exceeds your monthly expenses. With each additional passive income source, your revenue finally exceeds your expenses, and you achieve genuine financial freedom.

b.   It enables you to focus on what you like doing rather than what pays the bills.

With more time comes greater flexibility of choice, which might allow you to build more meaningful relationships with people and the world. Earnings from a passive income may enable you to explore your hobbies or contribute to humanitarian initiatives to enhance society, resulting in more contentment and a higher quality of life. It also liberates you from struggling to earn a living and instead follow your passion.

When your passive income exceeds your bills, why not become involved in a cause that you are passionate about? Perhaps you'd want to volunteer at a downtown homeless shelter that can't pay you. Perhaps you want to give your neighbor's kid a computer programming lessons, but they can't afford to pay you much. Whatever it is, you can do it because you are not concerned about your income.

c.   Reduces anxiety and stress

Passive income may provide stability and ease the stress of being unable to pay expenses. Passive income provides financial support and future security, resulting in the financial momentum to manage yourself, your time, and your possessions. It is difficult to be in the moment when we are terrified of the future.

Because we're so preoccupied with apocalyptic scenarios, it's difficult to appreciate what we have today. We're so concerned about an approaching fiscal catastrophe that it's difficult to break free from that line of thinking. It consumes and eats you. It's difficult to move away from it when it's all you can think about.

d.   It serves as a foundation for financial stability and development.

The financial security provided by passive income may enable you to retire earlier or more comfortably, as well as allow for financial development. Focusing on increasing your wealth rather than trying to maintain your present standard of living might bring financial clarity and help you reach your financial objectives more rapidly.

When you're not being tugged in so many ways, it's simpler to concentrate your attention on your money. While financial and other challenges will continue to emerge in your life, you will be better equipped to cope with them. You may focus your mind's eye on the things that will give you more development and wealth over time without the responsibility of hurrying off to a job you detest every single day.

The financial security provided by passive income may enable you to retire early.

e.   It allows you to live and work from anywhere.

Passive income may provide flexibility in your life, such as the ability to work from any place, making it simpler to travel or pursue other interests while maintaining your level of living. When you have a passive income, you can take a trip to any place you want at any time. You may live and work in Tokyo, Sydney, Rio de Janeiro, or almost any other city around the globe.

Whatever perspective you choose, the value of passive income cannot be overstated. Many individuals dismiss it because they don't comprehend it or believe that generating passive income that surpasses your expenses is unattainable. Well, the mind can accomplish anything it thinks.

That applies to passive income just as much as it does to everything else in life. You can do anything if you believe. So long as you don't quit.

What to Expect from the Book

Thank you for purchasing **"A Crash Course on Affiliate Marketing: A Comprehensive Beginner's Guide to Building Massive Passive Income by Leveraging the Most Lucrative Niches."** You should expect a transforming learning experience as you navigate the world of affiliate marketing.

Part A: Navigating Your Learning Path

Chapter 1: Understanding Affiliate Marketing

Begin your affiliate marketing adventure by knowing the fundamentals of the idea. Discover its history, present trends, and critical position in the digital ecosystem.

Chapter 2: Getting Started

Set reasonable objectives, cultivate a positive mentality, and understand the foundations of web marketing to lay the framework for your success.

Chapter 3: Building Your Foundation

Study the important factors of choosing a successful niche, defining your target audience, and making educated decisions about the affiliate products you promote.

Part B: Crafting Your Online Presence

Chapter 4: Creating a Strong Online Presence

Learn how to create a unique website or blog, optimize it for search engines, and use social media platforms to boost your affiliate marketing efforts.

Chapter 5: Crafting Compelling Content

Learn the significance of creating high-quality content, such as effective product reviews, interesting blog entries, and articles that connect with your target audience.

Chapter 6: Mastering the Art of Promotion

Investigate numerous promotional tactics, such as email marketing, social media marketing, and paid advertising choices.

Part C: Navigating the Affiliate Landscape

Chapter 7: Understanding Affiliate Networks

Navigate the affiliate network marketplace, learn popular ones, and maximize your revenues by selecting the right programs.

Chapter 8: Analyzing and Improving Performance

Dive into analytics tools, monitoring and assessing campaign results, and altering plans for continual optimization.

Chapter 9: Scaling Your Affiliate Marketing Business

Learn how to grow your company by outsourcing tasks, extending your product line, and diversifying revenue sources for long-term success.

Part D: Overcoming Challenges and Looking Ahead

Chapter 10: Overcoming Challenges

Give yourself the skills you need to overcome obstacles, cope with rejection and disappointments, and remain inspired throughout your affiliate marketing journey.

Conclusion

Recap essential principles, be encouraged to continue your success, and investigate the next stages in your fascinating affiliate marketing experience.

Appendix

To help you continue your education, look into other resources, tools, and a terminology of affiliate marketing jargon.

Prepare to discover the secrets of affiliate marketing and begin on a quest to create massive passive income. Let us begin!

Part A: Navigating Your Learning Path

Chapter 1: Understanding Affiliate Marketing

Begin your affiliate marketing adventure by knowing the fundamentals of the idea. Discover its historical history, present trends, and critical position in the digital ecosystem.

Chapter 2: Getting Started

Set reasonable objectives and cultivate a positive mentality,to lay the framework for your success.

Chapter 3: Building Your Foundation

Study the important factors of choosing a successful niche, defining your target audience, and making educated decisions about the affiliate products you promote.

Chapter 1: Understanding Affiliate Marketing

"Affiliate marketing has made businesses millions and ordinary people millionaires." - Bo Bennett

Definition and Concept

Almost everyone love to do their shopping online. Shopping at home is the most convenient option. Most people appreciate it since they don't have to travel to physical shops and because the products are offered at lower prices because companies save on shop expenses, resulting in lower total pricing.

But is that it? Most people are unaware that there is a lot more going on in the background than we realize. Here comes the notion of affiliate marketing, which is one of the quickest ways for a newbie to make money in the business sector. Affiliate marketing is the method by which a person known as an affiliate promotes a company's product or service.

The affiliate serves as a salesman on behalf of the company. As a result, the affiliate receives a commission once each targeted activity is completed. The intended activity differs in every business, and it is always agreed upon in advance. For example, it may be mailing list sign-ups, subscriptions, website clicks, or purchases.

Now, let's look at four concepts that are important to affiliate marketing.

a.   Performance Basis

Performance-based marketing is the foundation of affiliate marketing. So much so that affiliate marketing is usually referred to as "performance marketing," and appropriately so. This implies that the company will only reimburse the marketer if they drive the intended action (whether it's a sale, a subscription, a download, or whatever the business hopes to achieve via this partnership).

a.   Aspect of Independence

The importance of independence cannot be overstated. It is critical to recognize that affiliates are "independent marketers." They decide which affiliate marketing programs to join and which to discontinue, how much time and effort to spend into each relationship, how to prioritize them, and so on.

While there are methods for companies to attract affiliates, there is almost no way to force them to do anything they do not want to do. They are not workers. They are actually self-employed marketers.

b.   Partnership Component

There is also a foundation for partnership. Affiliate marketing programs are based on two factors under this framework: partnership with brands and independent affiliates (on content production, coordinated marketing efforts, and much more). Acknowledging affiliate independence puts the partnership aspect into context. Both "main players" are now equal, and there is no space for top-down approaches, just partnership.

c.   Universality

It is critical to recognize that "affiliate marketing" is not a "marketing channel," as many people believe. I labeled it "a way for businesses to partner with independent marketers" since it encompasses all types of marketing channels. A paid search marketer, a social media marketer, an email marketer, and even a real newspaper or radio station might become affiliates.

Types of affiliates is a different discussion, but it is important to understand and respect the universality of affiliate marketing: it works across channels. It doesn't matter what channel of marketing they use as long as the performance can be measured (and ascribed to the referring affiliate).

Historical Overview

PC Flowers and Gifts, an online flower company established by William J. Tobin, pioneered the first web affiliate network. The e-commerce site went online in 1989, and it quickly adopted an innovative marketing strategy. By 1993, the program was producing millions of dollars in sales each year. By 1995, it had over 2,500 affiliates from all over the internet.

Tobin sought for a patent on affiliate marketing and tracking in 1996. He received the patent in 2000. However, PC Flowers and Gifts was far from being the only participant on the affiliate marketing scene at the time. Other businesses saw its effectiveness and chose to employ the strategy too. Amazon happens to be one of those companies.

Amazon Enters the Market in 1996

Amazon Associates, the company's well-known affiliate program, debuted in 1996. Although it was not the first affiliate program, it was the first that was open to the general public. Members who signed up for Amazon Associates creates personalized banners that connected back to Amazon or directly to it. The program is now an unstoppable juggernaut.

For more than two decades, Amazon's growth has been spectacular. Amazon Associates may have contributed to some of their success. With affiliate networks sprouting up all over the place, Wayne Marciano founded Refer-it.com in 1997. This became the first Affiliate Program

Directory, providing an overview of the major affiliate networks to both affiliates and merchants.

A year later, AssociatePrograms.com, AffiliateGuide.com, ReveNews.com, and others published information and articles with affiliate directories. The United States Federal Trade Commission issued disclosure standards for affiliate marketing in 2000. The "Dot Com Disclosures: Information About Online Advertising" laws aided in the validity of affiliate marketing in the field of online marketing.

In 2008, the regulation was revised to require bloggers to reveal their affiliation with the businesses they promote. The 2001 dot.com bubble crash brought about substantial changes in affiliate marketing.

The frenzy of online business ventures that had been built during the commercial rise of the internet (dubbed the dot com boom) came crashing down in early 2000 when business fundamentals reasserted themselves, causing technology stocks to lose 60% of their value in just one year and bringing many back down to reality.

Online fortunes were no longer guaranteed. Internet marketers realized that in order to thrive in the sector, they needed to learn, research, and become experts in their subject. Affiliate marketing guidelines started to flood online bookstores, and the 'secrets' of affiliate marketing were made available to anybody willing to pay for them.

Missy Ward and Shawn Collins created Affiliate Summit in 2003 with the goal of educating affiliate marketers on the most recent industry developments and concerns, as well as creating a fruitful networking atmosphere for affiliate marketers. The inaugural Affiliate Summit in New York attracted 200 participants and is still going strong today.

Affiliate networks were predicted to generate roughly £2.16 billion in income in the United Kingdom alone by 2006, with global revenues anticipated to exceed $6.5 billion. Gambling, travel, personal finance, telecommunications, gaming, retail, and lead generation generated the majority of this money. According to an Internet Advisory Bureau (IAB) report, affiliate marketing accounted for 6% of the UK's total online economy in 2012 and generated £9 billion in sales.

Affiliate networks were predicted to generate roughly £2.16 billion in income in the United Kingdom

Affiliate marketing is very popular and continues to provide enormous potential, particularly as more and more online shops outperform their traditional counterparts. It's doubtful that customers will ever stop desiring information and doing research before buying a product or service, which is one of the key reasons why affiliate marketing is still thriving.

Evolution and Current Trends

Affiliate marketing is continuously evolving, and being up to date on the newest trends is critical to staying ahead of the competition. Here are some of today's top affiliate marketing trends:

a. Increased usage of artificial intelligence

In 2023, we are firmly in the thick of an AI revolution. With the introduction of generative AI technologies like ChatGPT, Midjourney, and Dall-e, people now have unparalleled access to creativity and productivity. Midjourney and Dall-e can produce graphics from natural language prompts, while ChatGPT uses natural language processing to generate human-like conversational text.

AI is making an impact on the affiliate marketing sector. Nothing will be left untouched in the next years, from content production and link building to website design and full-scale campaign creation.

b.   Increased Focus on Content Marketing

Many successful affiliate marketing campaigns now rely heavily on content marketing. By creating high-quality, relevant content, affiliate marketers can attract and engage their target audience, build confidence and trust, and ultimately boost sales. With the advent of social media and other digital platforms, content marketing is more important than ever.

c.   Mobile Affiliate Marketing is Expanding

Affiliate marketing has evolved in response to the increasing importance of mobile devices in our everyday lives. Mobile affiliate marketing is the promotion of goods and services using mobile channels such as mobile websites, mobile apps, and SMS marketing. Because of the expansion of mobile commerce, mobile affiliate marketing is expected to increase significantly in the future years.

Affiliate marketers can attract and engage their target audience using content marketing

d. Influencer Marketing's Emergence

Micro and nano influencers are social media profiles having a following of 1,000 to 50,000 people. In layman's terms, a nano/micro-influencer has more followers than the average individual but not enough to be termed a celebrity or a mega influencer. For quite some time, companies have been drawn to nano/micro influencers.

This is due to their increased contact with and influence over their followers. This, in turn, may lead to a higher conversion rate than bigger handles, which may struggle to convert. As influencers gain millions of followers and become superstars, they often lose their relatability and genuineness.

Audiences quickly realize that they are merely hawking a plethora of products, much like sports, models, or movie stars. On Instagram, for example, as the quantity of sponsored feeds increases, viewer engagement levels plummet.

d. Affiliate Network Evolution

Affiliate networks are platforms that link affiliate marketers with companies who have affiliate programs. These networks have been around for a while, but they have developed dramatically in recent years.

There are various affiliate networks available today, including some that specialize in certain sectors or industries. Furthermore, some affiliate networks have begun to provide extra services such as influencer marketing and mobile optimization.

e. Coupons, Promo Codes, and Cashback Will Prevail

Coupons and cashbacks have been and will continue to be a pillar of the affiliate marketing business in 2023. These are used by affiliate marketers to entice their audience to purchase a brand's products. They are also one of the most straightforward methods of attribution since they do not depend on cookies.

Affiliates often have specific discount codes or coupons, and when a client uses one of these codes to purchase, a company may simply connect the transaction to the relevant affiliate. Discounts and cashbacks will also become more important in 2024, given the global economy's overall recessionary signs.

Inflation and a prolonged period of economic downturn are having an impact on both large corporations and ordinary customers. In the second half of 2022, for example, inflation in the United States will reach levels not seen since at least the 1980s.

Affiliate Marketing Predictions for the Future

While affiliate marketing has gone a long way in the last several decades, there is always space for advancement and innovation. Here are some forecasts regarding affiliate marketing in the future:

a.   Use of video content is becoming more popular.

Recently, video material has surged in popularity. It is expected that affiliate marketing will depend on it more and more. By creating entertaining and useful video content, affiliate marketers can attract and engage their target audience, build confidence and trust, and finally boost sales.

b.   Niche Affiliate Marketing is on the rise.

As affiliate marketing evolves, we predict a greater emphasis on specialty marketing. By focusing on certain niches or sectors, affiliate marketers may tailor their campaigns to the needs and interests of their target audience.

c.   Increased Social Media Integration

We predict that social media will be used even more in the future, since it has become an important component of many great affiliate marketing tactics. Using the power of social media, affiliate marketers may reach a larger audience and connect with their target audience more directly.

d. Cross-Channel Marketing Growth

As the digital marketing landscape evolves, we expect to see a rise in affiliate marketers using cross-channel marketing. To build a unified and compelling brand presence, this method requires smoothly integrating numerous marketing channels such as social media, email campaigns, and content marketing.

Affiliate marketers may increase their reach, interact with varied audiences, and improve their methods for a more complete and successful promotional strategy by employing cross-channel marketing. As digital platforms become more linked, understanding cross-channel marketing will be critical for keeping ahead in the fast-paced world of affiliate marketing.

e. Creation of New Payment Models

New payment mechanisms for affiliate marketing are expected to emerge. Although the traditional commission-based model remains popular, there are various other payment methods available, such as pay-per-click, pay-per-lead, and pay-per-sale. As affiliate marketing evolves, we expect to see more testing of alternative payment options.

Chapter 2: Getting Started

"Someone's sitting in the shade today because someone planted a tree a long time ago." – Warren Buffett

Setting Realistic Goals

Affiliate marketers supply a variety of companies with high-traffic advertising space on the Internet. It has grown in popularity as Web technology have advanced, allowing marketers to draw greater audiences to websites with a range of adverts.

Ambitious affiliate marketers, who are generally self-employed, create goals and objectives on a regular basis to assist them to succeed. Examining a few popular affiliate marketing objectives might help you grasp what it takes to thrive in this rapidly growing sector.

a.   Revenue Goals

The ultimate purpose of every affiliate marketing program is to generate income, and effective affiliate marketers establish short and long-term income targets to motivate them to constantly improve the value of their services. Affiliate marketing companies may be compensated in a variety of ways, including when a website visitor clicks on an advertising or when a click results in a sale. Affiliate marketers might create targets to balance the sorts of payments they receive and the dates they are paid by various advertisers in order to maintain a consistent and rising income stream.

b. Cost and Profitability Goals

Affiliate marketing businesses operate on a lean company model, often handling all operations from a home office with the owner as the single employee. Setting cost-cutting targets may help affiliate marketers capitalize on this edge, bringing in more money without raising overhead or labor expenditures. Choosing the correct Internet service provider, finding the right website hosts, and designing websites on your own may all help you save money and reach your profit targets.

c. Traffic Goals

Web traffic might be an affiliate marketer's most valuable asset, enabling them to recruit high-paying customers rather than cold-calling, email blasts, and other time-consuming business-to-business marketing tactics. Affiliate marketers may use website analytics tools to measure how many people arrive through each website each day, as well as where each visitor is situated. Setting objectives for affiliate website geographic reach as well as overall traffic flowing into various assets on a daily basis may lead straight to better earnings.

d. Productivity Goals

In the early phases of affiliate marketing, sales may be critical, and establishing daily productivity objectives can help businesses succeed in acquiring their first customers. Bringing in visitors in the early phases of an affiliate website may also be difficult, requiring some vigilance on the side of the marketers.

Affiliate marketers may create productivity goals such as publishing a particular number of informative contents on their websites each month, producing a specific number of articles or blog posts each week, chasing a certain number of advertising customers each week, or any other productivity-related target.

Web traffic enables affiliates to recruit high-paying customers

Creating a Positive Mindset

You must build your organizing and critical thinking abilities in order to achieve the correct affiliate attitude and conquer the problems that come your way. A successful affiliate marketer need more than just technical competence and marketing plan knowledge. A positive mindset and approach are also required.

a.   Believe In Yourself

The first golden rule of goal setting in affiliate marketing is to believe that you can accomplish what you are about to start doing. Allow no one or any event to bring you or your desired affiliate marketing approach down. There are several affiliate marketing options available for you to pursue, as well as lots of money to be made.

Be aware that the number of successful affiliate marketers grows by the minute, and you may be one of them. Yes, believe in yourself, and you will achieve the biggest goal you have ever set for yourself in your whole life. However, you are sure to hit some marketing stumbling blocks, but if you stick with it and believe in what you are doing, you will be the next affiliate marketer millionaire in no time.

b.   Persistence

Because affiliate marketing is not a get-rich-quick scheme, perseverance is essential. To build a successful affiliate business, you must invest time, effort, and dedication. Despite the fact that many great affiliates met hurdles and failures along the road, they persevered and moved on. Adopt a tenacious mentality and be willing to put in the necessary work to achieve your objectives.

Adopt a tenacious mentality and be willing to put in the necessary work to achieve your objectives.

c. Continuous Education

Staying static in this fast changing sector is not an option. A growth mentality that values constant learning and improvement is your ticket to success. It motivates you to experiment with new tactics, methods, and trends, as well as to adapt to changing market situations. A dedication to lifelong learning keeps you at the forefront of innovation.

d. Creativity

Effective affiliate marketers think creatively and build unique ideas to promote products and attract customers. Rather than depending only on traditional marketing methods, seek for unique perspectives and approaches that will set you apart from the competition. Experiment with different marketing platforms, content genres, and promotional techniques to see what works best for your audience.

e. Resilience

Digital and affiliate marketing may be difficult, with many ups and downs. Your capacity to recover from failures, adjust to changes, and keep going demonstrates your resilience. Failures may be seen as learning opportunities rather than dead ends if you have a resilient mentality. This viewpoint may assist you in growing, refining your plans, and finally achieving your objectives.

f. Relationship Development

Relationship building with your audience and business partners is a crucial aspect of affiliate marketing. Develop a relations with your audience by providing useful information, communicating with them, and catering to their needs. Connect with other affiliate marketers, thought leaders, and industry experts. Collaborations, partnerships, and information sharing may extend your horizons and open up new doors.

g. Goal-setting

Setting specific, attainable objectives is critical in digital and affiliate marketing. Your mentality should allow you to identify your goals, break them down into doable actions, and remain committed to achieving them. Goal-oriented thinking holds you responsible, motivates you, and gives you a feeling of purpose.

h. Be Creative

Affiliate marketing is not for marketers who copy and paste since it will make you lazy. And, as you know, lazy individuals seldom build a name for themselves. You will need to be more innovative and unique in your marketing methods than your competition. You cannot expect to generate substantial money from affiliate marketing by just using the same marketing method that you employed two years ago.

For example, if you employed written content to sell your affiliate product last year, you cannot anticipate different results this year. You must refresh your written content using the appropriate terms and marketing phrases. Changing your marketing strategy can allow you to enter new markets and sell more things than you ever imagined.

This is particularly true if the product offers several advantages. You'll hit all of the appropriate selling points. And after you've done that, you'll understand what it implies for your affiliate revenue.

Chapter 3: Building Your Foundation

"Affiliate marketing isn't about commissions; it's about helping people find the value they are looking for." – –
Shivansh Bhanwariya

Selecting a Profitable Niche

It's no secret that choosing the correct niche is essential if you want to succeed in affiliate marketing. It is critical to the success of your affiliate company. Your affiliate specialty dictates what you market and who you target.

If you want to make a lot of money, you should invest in a niche that has a lot of demand but little competition. But wait, there's more! It's also critical to choose a specialization that is related to your interests or hobbies.

As Captain Obvious may say, promoting something you care about makes the whole process more enjoyable and fulfilling. You're more inclined to remain with it over time. It is critical to do thorough research and select the most successful affiliate marketing areas. It will make or break your ability to develop a profitable and sustained affiliate company.

When selecting an affiliate marketing niche, bear in mind that you want to make money in the long run. Trending subjects or items might generate large earnings while they persist, but they generally pass away, leaving you to hunt again. Having said that, there is no one-size-fits-all solution for determining the most successful affiliate marketing areas.

Every marketer has diverse areas of interest and experience that may have a significant impact on their effectiveness. While one person may have had tremendous success in an unusual niche, another person may have made a fortune in a conventional specialty. What is incredibly lucrative for someone else may not necessarily be advantageous for you.

However, there are key considerations that every affiliate marketer should consider while deciding on a niche.

a.   Low competition

A low-competition topic is a good place to start for inexperienced affiliate marketers. Your audience will only find your affiliate content if you can outrank the currently existing content at the top of Search Engine Results Pages (SERPs). There are certain categories where the top-ranking sites are difficult to outperform.

They may be very authoritative or have exceptionally powerful SEO, particularly if they are established and popular websites with large budget. A new entrant would have a tough time competing in such a niche. That is why it is critical to begin with a niche with low competition.

You might seek for niches where the top-ranking content isn't as authoritative and where you have the opportunity to create affiliate content that provides more value to the audience than what the top sites are providing.

a.   High level of interest

You must also guarantee that the niche you choose is of high interest, which indicates that the target market's audience is interested in it. A niche may have little competition but also little appeal, in which case your attempts to create affiliate marketing content will be futile. As a result, it is critical to discover what individuals in your target market are looking for and want to know about.

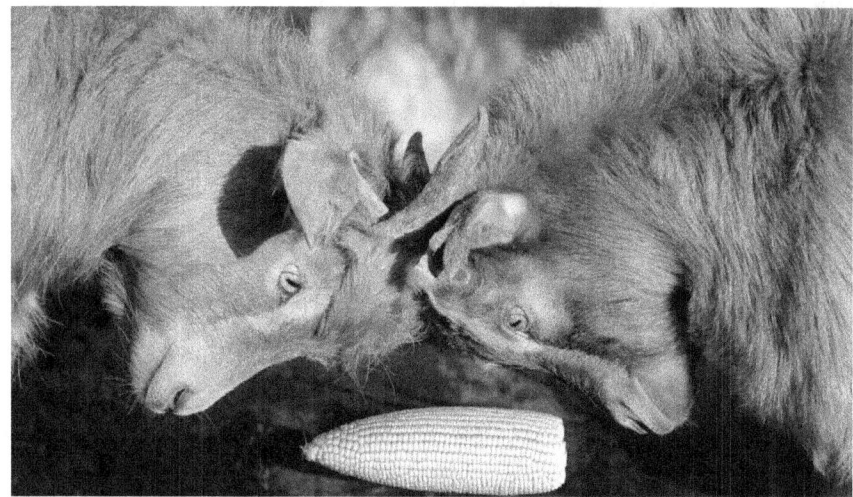

A new entrant would have a tough time competing with sites at the top of SERPs

High-interest niches are likely to have significantly more competition since all affiliate marketers want to work in these popular areas. The trick here is to find a happy medium between competitiveness and interest. Look for something with little competition yet a large fan base.

You might even branch out from a popular specialty into something nearly similar. That manner, you may be able to generate the same level of interest in individuals while still avoiding competition since not many affiliate marketers have written content on the subject. For example, if smartphones are a high-interest, high-competition niche, you may go outside the box and search for something similar - such as smart home devices or Bluetooth products - that are relatively low competition but popular.

b.   Monetization

The goal of affiliate marketing is to make money from the information you develop and distribute. If you want to monetise your blog or other content channels, there are hundreds of affiliate programs to choose from. Not all of them are equally lucrative.

As a result, it is critical that you choose a topic with reputable and successful affiliate networks. Another thing to consider is the affiliate platform's conversion rates. A platform with high commissions but low conversions may nonetheless be less lucrative than one with lower commissions but higher conversion guarantees.

Amazon is a fantastic example. Amazon decreased income for affiliate program members drastically in April 2021, yet due to the program's strong conversion rates, affiliate marketers still find it useful. Visitors may not necessarily purchase the product they clicked on your affiliate site, but they may end up purchasing something else that earns you a commission.

As a result, it is critical to ensure that your affiliate marketing niche includes markets and goods that can generate traffic and earnings.

c.   Longevity

There may be certain affiliate marketing niches that are incredibly successful right now and seem to be a great match. But how long will these gains last? When launching an affiliate marketing business, you must plan for the long term.

Certain products, servicesand programs are only available for a short time. As previously stated, most popular niches or products have an expiration period. Seasonal products, for example, are only available for the duration of the season.

Advertising for certain Christmas products is fleeting. Similarly, if you are marketing an event or event-related items, your affiliate campaigns will be ineffective until the event has concluded. These may be useful as a side business, but when it comes to affiliate marketing niches, you want to choose ones that are evergreen.

Select products, sectors, and platforms that will outlast the competition. The sustainability of your topic is important if you want to generate long-term income from affiliate marketing.

d.   Interest

Finally, the most significant factor to consider is your area of interest. You might select a high-interest, low-competition, evergreen niche available, but you will never attain the results you want unless you are driven to work on it. Choosing a niche that actually interests you is much more crucial than chasing profits.

Even if the affiliate marketing topic you choose is low-profit, your enthusiasm for it will drive you to work harder on it on a continuous basis, and such tenacity will undoubtedly generate rewards. Affiliate marketing involves both time and effort. Creating high-quality affiliate marketing content that converts might be difficult if you lose interest in your job or have to push yourself too hard.

It will be easy to choose an affiliate marketing specialty now that you know what it should look like. But, as with anything else, there is a process behind it. You may guarantee that you make a careful and well-thought-out choice by following these simple steps:

a.   **Begin by determining your areas of interest and competence.**

Because your enthusiasm in the niche will be one of the most important elements to examine, it is essential to begin by selecting your areas of interest. Do you have any specific expertise? Are you especially interested in a certain subject because of a passion or a skill? For instance, if you have a background in user interface/user experience (UI/UX) design or electronics, you may excel at comprehending and articulating information about gadgets, smartphones, smartwatches, computers, and similar devices to your audience.

Alternatively, if you are a cosmetics fan with extensive knowledge of products and trends, you might educate your audience about beauty products by providing honest affiliate product reviews. Identifying your calling narrows things down and makes future decisions much simpler. Furthermore, if you already have some background and understanding in the selected area, writing affiliate marketing content will be much easier for you.

b.   **Brainstorm ideas for these topics of interest.**

Once you've determined your area of interest, you can begin brainstorming ideas. Look for products related to your interests for which you may generate affiliate marketing conent. You must look for items or services in which costumers are interested.

There are a few tools available for this. Google Trends is a handy, free tool for doing preliminary research. It displays current trending searches based on the terms or subjects you provide. For example, the subject 'chatgpt' showed what individuals searched for in connection to it in the last 12 months, as seen below.

The subject 'chatgpt' showed what individuals searched for in connection to it in the last 12 months

A fast search on Amazon is another approach to find out what products are available in your area of interest. Amazon product listings are divided into various categories and subcategories. You may want to consider products with positive ratings in the category that aligns with your concept, as these are often of interest to customers. Depending on your objectives, you can then apply criteria such as price, brand, and other relevant factors.

c.   Determine the niche's profitability.

With this preliminary study, you are well on your way to deciding on an affiliate marketing niche. However, even if you know what products/services you can promote, you need also learn about the affiliate programs with which they are linked. Research which affiliate networks you may join for each topic to test your ideas.

Then you must learn how these affiliate schemes pay. You must choose a topic with adequate, reputable affiliate networks that will provide you with a reasonable opportunity of generating high cash. A Google search for your niche keywords + affiliate program should provide some interesting results. Consider the following example.

You must check that affiliate programs for the niche give decent commissions, a diverse choice of products to promote, and a sizable user base. A strong affiliate program should also provide its associates with enough resources and tools to help them learn on a constant basis.

A Google search for your specialty keywords + affiliate program should provide some interesting results

d.   Examine the niche's search volumes and competitiveness.

You should also do niche research to evaluate how your selected niche performs in terms of user interest and competition. Though we have previously said that low competition niches are the ideal to begin with, this does not imply that you should choose a niche in which none of your competitors desire to explore. If this is the case, it is quite probable that there is no audience interest in the niche as well. You'll need a niche with large search volumes and competitors ready to explore.

This is when a basic keyword search tool like SEMrush or Google Keyword Planner might come in handy. Simply enter a broad term relating to the selected subject, and the program will provide a plethora of other similar keywords that will tell you what people often seek for in this area. It also displays keyword difficulty, which indicates how tough it might be to rank for certain keywords in search results in attempt to outperform the top sites in SERP.

Tools like SEMrush or Google Keyword Planner helps in examining niche's search volumes and competitiveness

The keyword search volume displays how many monthly searches the term gets on average. You may also examine the terms' Cost Per Click (CPC). CPC is the price advertisers are ready to pay for a single keyword click. This suggests that keywords with a high CPC are preferred.

e.   Look for areas where the affiliate marketing content in the niche could be improved.

The last stage in establishing your niche is deciding whether there is room to provide additional value to the audience. If you choose a popular niche, there will almost probably be existing affiliate content in that area. Even the finest marketers are prone to making affiliate content blunders from time to time.

You must identify the gaps that you can fill. One of the greatest ways to assure success in your affiliate marketing area is to provide something that no one else offers. You must generate affiliate content that is new, distinctive, and highly relevant.

This will, however, need some work. Study the content on the top-ranking websites in your niche and make a note of everything they have failed to provide. Once you've done that for the top 10 or 15 websites, you can devise a plan for outperforming them.

It might be some important information, the experience provided by the content, or anything else that can be improved. If you can't locate any, this is probably not the proper niche for you. By the conclusion of this stage, you should have a plan if you can identify gaps to fill.

Identifying Target Audiences

Understanding and targeting your affiliate marketing audience is critical for success in the ever-changing world of internet marketing. When it comes to advertising goods or services via affiliate networks, understanding your target audience's tastes, requirements, and habits may have a huge influence on the success of your campaign. You may customize your marketing efforts to correspond with your audience's preferences by analyzing data and getting insights into their demographics, interests, and buying behavior, thus raising your chances of generating conversions and optimizing your affiliate marketing earnings.

Understanding your affiliate marketing audience is critical to the success of your efforts. Knowing your audience allows you to personalize your content and promotions to their interests and preferences. For example, if your target audience is predominantly made up of young millennials interested in fashion, pushing the newest apparel trends and giving unique discounts would almost certainly provide greater results than advertising home décor items.

Understanding your audience allows you to find possible niches or subgroups within your target market that you may have missed before. This insight enables you to build targeted campaigns for certain segments of your audience, increasing your chances of success.

Here are five ways to identify the right technique to define your target audience:

a. **Study your current audience.**

Learn about their existing purchasing habits, feedback, product interaction, and what they love doing online, such as social media, blogs, forums, news, and so on. The following are the most popular methods for doing this analysis:

- **Social media analytics**: Track comments, interaction, new page likes, and so on.

- **Google Analytics**: Track and identify your audience, which is comprised of segments with distinct interests, intent, demographics, channels, behavioral data, and so on.

Study your current audience

b.   **Determine the challenges that your product or service addresses.**

Identify the problem or the pain point that needs to be solved. Understanding the problems of existing and potential customers and empathizing with them will help you to identify valuable insights about their motivations and interests.

c.   **Segment your target market**

After reviewing the previous two phases, you should have a clearer idea of your target audience. It is now time to establish the suitable demographics for your products in order to reach your target audience via digital media channels. Understanding your audience's gender, age, and interests allows you to define the kind of media you need to generate.

d.   **Research your competitors**

Research what other affiliate marketers are doing to sell your kind of product or a comparable product to learn about their strategy and viewpoint. Learn about their target demographic, advertising strategies, and distinctive selling points. Understanding your competition allows you to uncover market gaps, fine-tune your own strategy, and develop a unique value proposition that sets you apart in the competitive environment.

Keep an eye on industry developments and assess your competitors' activity on a regular basis to change your affiliate marketing strategy for long-term success.

e.   Gather extensive information about your target audience.

It's now time to compile the information you gathered when establishing your target audience. Put everything together and make certain that all necessary information is included.

Choosing the Right Affiliate Products

Affiliate marketing enables you to make money by advertising items and services that you believe in and are relevant to your target audience. Choosing the correct affiliate products to promote, on the other hand, may be a difficult undertaking. Here are five pointers to help you choose the best affiliate products.

a.   Understand Your Audience

Understanding your audience is essential for selecting the best affiliate products. You must understand your audience's interests, needs, and pain areas. Conducting market research and evaluating your social media statistics may help you acquire insight into your audience's demographics, interests, and activity. This data will assist you in selecting affiliate products that are relevant to your audience and likely to be purchased.

b.   Promote businesses you believe in.

Before you market any company's product, you must ensure that your fundamental values fit with the company's basic values. If there is an obvious disparity between your brand's mission and theirs, it will not seem like a natural fit to your audience. Some bloggers have made the mistake of collaborating with companies that have a negative public image, and their influence has suffered as a result of selling their products.

The simplest method to avoid this is to do thorough study before expressing an interest in partnering or becoming an affiliate. It's an excellent strategy to safeguard yourself and your own brand. Typically, you may discover more about a company by reading their About page or digging further into their blog content to see what they value.

When in doubt, contact the company's contact for further information. They'll be impressed that you inquired.

c.   Look for Products of High Quality.

When selecting affiliate products to market, make sure they are of excellent quality. Your target audience wants you to propose goods that are both valuable and satisfy their requirements. If you advocate low-quality items, your audience will lose faith in you and be less inclined to buy the things you suggest in the future.

d.   Take into account the Commission Rate

As an affiliate, your commission rate is the proportion of the sale that you made. You should choose products with a reasonable commission rate. However, you should not be only concerned with the commission rate. A high-quality product with a lower commission rate is preferable than a low-quality product with a higher commission rate. Your first objective should be to deliver value to your audience, with the commission as a secondary concern.

e.   Study the Affiliate Program Terms

It is critical to read and comprehend the affiliate program's terms and conditions before marketing any affiliate products. You must follow all laws and regulations, including declaring your affiliate arrangement with your target audience. You should also make certain that the program has a fair and clear commission structure, gives assistance, and pays on schedule.

Part B: Crafting Your Online Presence

Chapter 4: Creating a Strong Online Presence

Learn how to create a unique website or blog, optimize it for search engines, and use social media platforms to boost your affiliate marketing efforts.

Chapter 5: Crafting Compelling Content

Learn the significance of creating high-quality content, such as effective product reviews, interesting blog entries, and articles that connect with your target audience.

Chapter 6: Mastering the Art of Promotion

Investigate numerous promotional tactics, such as email marketing, social media marketing, and paid advertising choices.

Chapter 4: Creating a Strong Online Presence

"Organic reach is so important because the impression you get when someone comes directly to your page is a much more qualified lead and potentially a more valuable customer than someone you got through an ad buy."

– Gary Vaynerchuk

Building Your Website or Blog

It is preferable to develop a niche website around a topic that people are enthusiastic about and ready to spend money on. You may also make an affiliate website for special occasions such as Halloween, Easter, Thanksgiving, and Christmas. This website allows you to market costumes and décor products.

Starting out as an affiliate publisher may be simpler than you think. You're halfway there if you have a laptop and access to the internet. In eight easy steps, here's how to get started.

a.   **Select a Topic**

To begin, consider what you want to write about. What is your pastime? What is your calling? Running, collecting toy robots, sewing, or planting hot peppers are all possibilities.

While these subjects may seem odd at first look, they are all suitable for an affiliate website. Niching down works well for affiliate marketing since it allows you to more easily:

- Determine your target audience's demographics.
- Address your audience's concerns.
- Establish authority on a subject

b.   Promote products that match the demands of your target audience

Above all, ensure that you are interested in the topic. You must develop articles on your topic on a regular basis. The greatest method to grow your website's readership is to write often and have a unique voice.

You're already one step ahead if you're currently developing content in a certain niche. Simply construct a website about your subject and fill it with information from other platforms, such as YouTube or a podcast.

c.   Select a Domain Name and a Web Hosting Service Provider

After deciding on the sort of website to create, acquire a web hosting package - a service that stores your website data online and makes it available to internet users. To create an affiliate website, you'll also need a domain name, which serves as the site URL that visitors put into their browser. Many web servers include domain name registration, eliminating the need to purchase both hosting and a domain separately.

For newbies, choosing the cheapest web host may be appealing. However, for better long-term website performance, I suggest investing in premium hosting.

Six considerations should be examined while selecting a web hosting provider:

- **Speed**. Choose a web host with a consistent and fast server speed to guarantee your website loads smoothly. Check its uptime guarantee and status - the higher the percentage, the better.

- **Security**. A competent web host should provide SSL certificates, frequent backups, and important security measures to keep viruses at bay.

- **User-friendliness**. To make it easier to set up a website, beginners should select a web host with an easy-to-use control panel.

- **Price.** Look for web hosting with low start-up and renewal fees. Depending on the type, web hosting may range from $2 to $500 per month.

- **Support**. Ascertain that the hosting firm offers 24-hour assistance to aid you if a problem arises.

- **Scalability**. Affiliate marketers should be able to upgrade their hosting plans as their website grows.

Many web servers provide varied deals, so choose a hosting plan that meets your requirements. For beginning, we suggest WordPress shared hosting since it is inexpensive and simple to maintain.

d. Figure Out Your Domain Name

A bespoke domain name is preferable than a free domain name that includes the name of the website provider. It's simple, concise, and lends credibility to a website. A decent domain should be brief, concise, and easy to spell, with three to four words at most.

Incorporating important keywords into a domain name may also assist visitors and search engines in determining the purpose of a website. Consider using a top-level domain for the chosen region if you have a particular audience in mind. For example, if you want to target Canadians, use the **.ca** domain and the **.es** domain to attract the Spanish market.

e. Choose a Platform for Your Website

The basis of creating a website is selecting the correct platform, since it will impact its appearance, functionality, user experience, and upkeep. Let's look at four things to think about while deciding on the ideal web platform for your affiliate marketing website:

- **Simple to use.** It is possible to create a full website without needing to comprehend or write code. However, other online platform interfaces may be better for some individuals to use, so explore and select what is best for you.
- **Customization.** Find a platform that allows you to customize the design and functions of your website depending on your requirements.
- **Price.** Examine the platform's price bundle and potential add-ons, then compare the results to your budget.
- **Support.** Check to see whether the platform provides help in the form of tutorials, forums, or emails.

There are two types of website platforms in general: content management systems (CMS) like WordPress and website builders. The primary difference between a WordPress and a website builder is that the former requires more time to learn but provides more flexibility and scalability, whilst the latter has an easy-to-use interface but restricted alternatives. Advanced features such as an affiliate management system and live chat assistance may be enabled via WordPress plugins.

Furthermore, there are several themes available to alter the design of the website to your liking. The initial step in using this platform is to install WordPress. The easiest option is to use an auto-installer from your hosting provider's control panel, if yours has one.

f. **Personalize Your Website**

Following the installation of the platform, the next step is to design the website and customize the features to fit your preferences and make the site more attractive. A visually appealing website may boost initial impressions and keep visitors interested.

- **Select a Theme**

A theme defines the overall appearance and feel of your website. It includes basic options that affect the look and functioning of your site, such as your logo, color scheme, and typography. WordPress's main theme directory has a plethora of free theme possibilities. Each WordPress theme has a unique layout and set of features for a particular purpose.

Alternatively, to obtain a distinctive look and better support, buy a premium WordPress theme. Make sure the theme you chose has a responsive layout. This implies that the theme can adjust to the user's device automatically.

After you've finished downloading the theme, I suggest that you install a few plugins to improve the functioning of your WordPress website. I recommend the following plugins to assist enhance the speed and security of your website

- **SEO plugins:** Increase traffic to your website by optimizing it for search engines. Use SEO plugins like Yoast SEO, RankMath, and AIOSEO.
- **Backup plugins:** While your hosting provider will take care of it, you may do periodic website backups by installing plugins. UpdraftPlus and WP Time Capsule are two popular ones.
- **Caching plugins:** Do you want to improve the speed of your website? WP Rocket, W3 Total Cache, and WP-Optimize are examples of caching plugins.
- **Security plugins:** Protect your WordPress website from viruses and cyber-attacks. WordFence, iThemes Security, and Sucuri are popular security plugins.

A typical affiliate marketing website will include a large number of affiliate links. Yes, it will also depend on how many things you promote, but you get the idea. While some links are brief, some are extensive and do not make for a professional-looking URL.

While there is a shorter version, the complete Amazon affiliate link will look something like this: https://www.amazon.com?&linkCode=ll2&tag=XXXXXXXXX-

21&linkId=9271806315844cbababf972b40981f20&language=en_IN&ref_=as_li_ss_tl,. Is it simple to remember? I guess not!

Here's another example. Assume the merchant modifies the affiliate link, which must then be changed throughout your website. If you simply have one or two pages on your website, upgrading those links will be simple.

It will be time-consuming, to say the least, if you have hundreds of pages! ThirstyAffiliates (thirstyaffiliates.com/) and Pretty Links (prettylinks.com/) are two plugins that may help with this. They enable you to hide URLs and show more user-friendly links. Instead of showing a long Amazon link, we can use these plugins to display a URL like https://domain.com/amazon.

When users click on the cloaked URL, they are forwarded to the actual link. When you wish to alter your links, just modify your cloaked URL, and the changes will be reflected throughout your website.

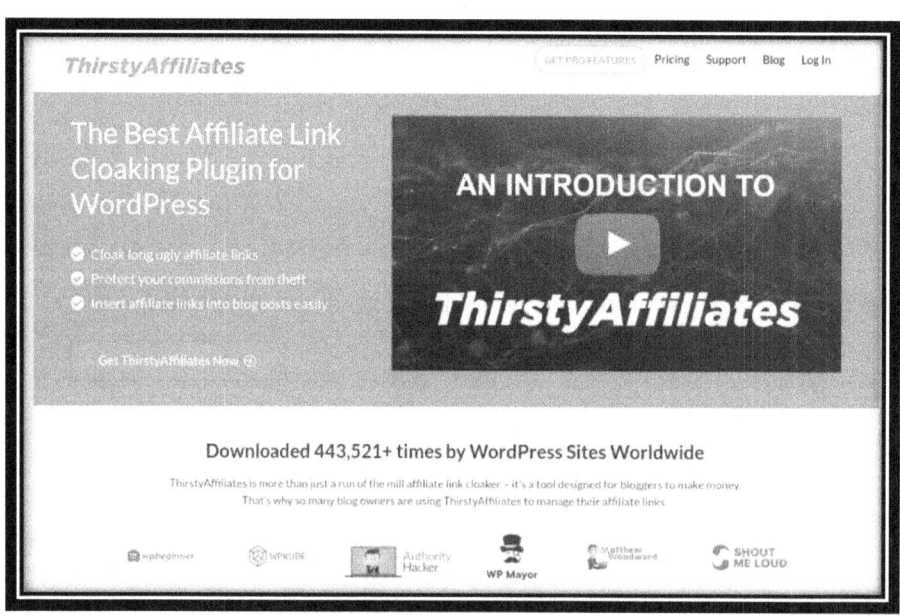

ThirstyAffiliates and Pretty Links are two plugins tha helps with links shortening and customization

a. Create content for your specialized niche.

It is now time to begin creating content. Blogging is an excellent approach to produce content for your website since you may write about topics that you are passionate about. You may also utilize your blog to provide tutorials and other forms of material to keep your audience interested.

What type of material should you be producing to distinguish yourself as a knowledgeable and trustworthy affiliate marketer?

Content Types to Produce

Here are some examples of content that works well for an affiliate marketing website.

Product reviews

Product reviews are an extremely powerful content marketing approach. Customers are always looking for useful information about different goods and services. Assume you write an amazing product review that highlights the different features, advantages, and instructions for using a product.

In such situation, you'll be teaching your audience and finally persuading them to buy the product.

Product comparisons

Are you making a comparison between two products? Consider reading the product A vs. product B comparison article. Product comparisons are most effective when customers are deciding between two products.

It's the last push before you make a buy. What if your content might assist clients in deciding which product to purchase? A well-written product comparison piece may do this.

As long as your content is relevant, you may generate passive revenue by incorporating affiliate links.

Best-of articles

The 'best of' articles are another kind of content that works well for affiliate marketing websites. You know, the greatest themes, plugins, and page builders, among other things. In such articles, you may list many products, their benefits and drawbacks, and help customers by providing an unbiased evaluation of the product.

Naturally, the call to action (CTA) for each product will be your affiliate link.

'How-to' manuals

Want to get a lot of traffic to your website even if you're just starting out? Make 'how-to' articles! How-to postings are informative and usually include a step-by-step explanation on how to utilize a certain product.

b.   Enroll in affiliate programs.

You've already reached the stage where you can begin joining up for affiliate programs, believe it or not. There are two methods to find and join affiliate programs.

Directly collaborate with a brand

Over 80% of marketers have an affiliate marketing program, so some of the brands or merchants you currently patronize may have their own. To see whether a brand has an active affiliate program, just Google the brand name and "affiliate program." A search for "Target affiliate program" will take you to partners.target.com.

The store fully defines its affiliate program, even down to the prospective compensation rate.

Participate in an affiliate program

While many firms provide simple sign-up forms directly on their websites, others aggressively solicit partners via affiliate programs. Amazon Associates runs one of the world's most well-known affiliate programs. Despite being the largest online retailer, Amazon does not pay the highest commissions.

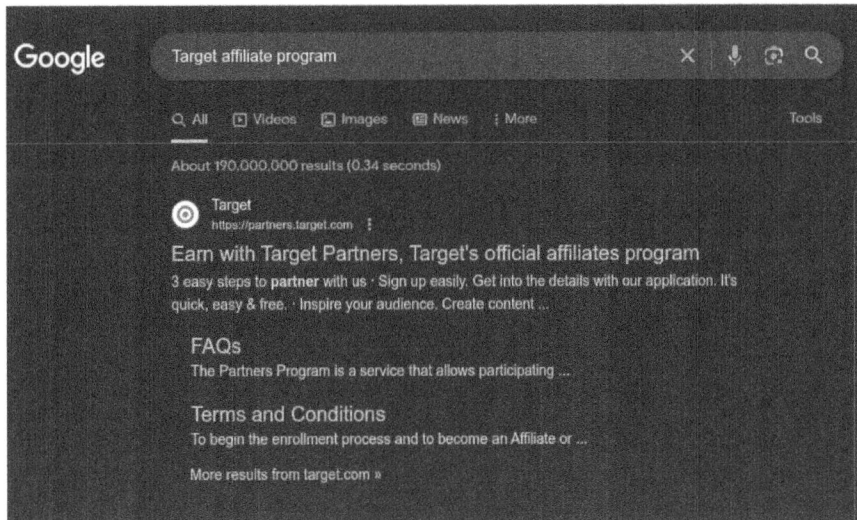

A search for "Target affiliate program" will take you to partners.target.com

Rates vary per product category, although the majority simply give single-digit commissions. Fortunately, organizations like as impact.com have established their businesses around administering affiliate programs for hundreds of brands, making it simple for both big and small affiliates to join up **impact.com** Marketplace. The impact.com Marketplace links you with products that are relevant to your interests.

This makes it easy to choose the ideal brand partner for your audience's products and services. Even better, these businesses often pay bigger fees than Amazon.

When you join a bigger affiliate platform, you will also be able to:

- Establish direct relationships with brands of your choice;
- Negotiate unique contract terms according to your requirements;
- Optimize your connections as your company grows.

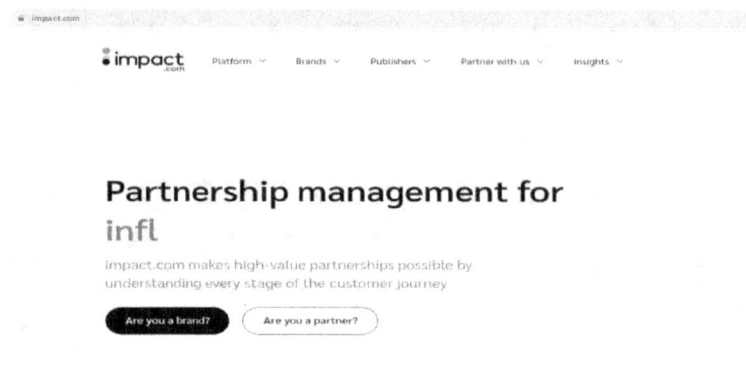

The impact.com Marketplace links you with products that are relevant to your interests.

c. Integrate affiliate links into your website.

It's time to start making money now that you've successfully joined a brand's affiliate program or an affiliate network! The majority of current affiliate programs are simple to use. Brands allow you to look through product listings and choose what you want to market.

Many affiliate marketers prefer bigger affiliate networks since they provide more product selections that may be suitable for your target audience. The brand will then offer you with automatic, tailored affiliate links to use in your article. Each link is personalized for you and contains affiliate tracking information.

When a reader clicks on the link, the brand knows you provided them traffic. When customers make a purchase on the site, you get a commission.

d. Increase visitors to your website.

Increased website traffic means more opportunity for profitable sales. Every sale implies higher commissions for you as an affiliate publisher. Even if these new visitors do not purchase anything via your link, you have captivated the interest of someone who may purchase in the future.

Make a strong content amplification plan. Invest in these organic marketing tactics to increase website visitors.

Methods for increasing visitors to your website

- **Make SEO a high priority.**

You may gain free, organic traffic to your website by choosing popular keywords that are relevant to your target demographic. The more money you put on organic search, the more visitors you'll get. According to BrightEdge data, organic search accounts for 53.3 percent of all online traffic, with the great majority of visitors only browsing through the first five results of their search.

Still not convinced? The value of investing in search-optimized content and other SEO initiatives is reflected in consumer behavior. According to a recent poll, 49 percent of buyers use Google to explore or locate a new service or product.

- **Keep an email list**

Email marketing still ranks as one of the greatest methods for affiliates to markets products, with an average return on investment (ROI) of $38 for every $1 invested. You always have an owned database of subscribers who chose to hear from you when you establish and manage a strong email list. Even if your email subscribers do not buy things directly from you, you may still profit from the traffic your emails send to your website.

- **Maintain an active presence on social media.**

Investigate which platforms your target audience prefers and create a profile on those channels. Social media may provide vital exposure for your content as well as visitors to your website. In 2023, internet users spent an average of 147 minutes per day on social media, and marketers cited improved visibility and traffic as two of the top social media marketing advantages.

Consider social media to be a marketing tool rather than your online home. Stay active and engage your audience by connecting to your content on a regular basis. Experiment with fresh methods to entice social media followers to leave the platform and visit your website, email list, or other owned assets.

Consider social media to be a marketing tool rather than your online home

- **Make guest posts**

Expand your reach by guest blogging on other websites in your field and connecting back to your own. Spending time writing content for someone else's website may seem contradictory, yet guest blogging may immediately enhance traffic by exposing your work to a new audience. Other benefits of guest posting include:

• Connecting with a larger audience and potentially gaining followers.

• Building bridges with other content creators.

• Establishing yourself as a thought leader in your niche.

• Growing domain authority and boosting SEO efforts.

e.   **Publish high-quality articles on a regular basis.**

Some products linked on your website may be featured by major publications with extensive websites. In today's competitive affiliate publishing environment, you must build an audience and win their trust by providing high-quality content that addresses their primary pain points. Create an editorial calendar to create smart, unique content on a regular basis.

Some methods for always coming up with subject ideas in your field include:

- Sharing answers to frequent problems that your audience faces
- Discussing fresh, relevant findings and trends
- Compiling roundups of products that target certain pain areas
- Comparing comparable products when they are introduced
- Highlighting success stories and case studies
- Creating seasonal content

Remember how I told you to create a few blogs and find your voice? That voice also gains the confidence of your audience. This trust drives people to click on the goods you promote and recommend, paving the way for more affiliate earnings.

Optimizing for Search Engines

Search Engine Optimization (SEO) refers to the process of increasing a website's visibility and rating in search engine results. The ultimate objective of SEO is to attract organic (non-paid) traffic from search engines such as Google, Bing, Yahoo, and others. When users search for certain keywords or phrases relating to a website's content, a well-optimized site has a greater chance of appearing higher in the search results, boosting the likelihood that visitors will click through to the site.

SEO's critical components include:

a. **Keyword Research:** Selecting and concentrating on relevant search phrases that prospective consumers are likely to use.

b. **On-Page Optimization**: Enhancing the website's relevance to search queries by optimizing the content, meta tags, headers, and URLs (uniform resource locators) to correlate with targeted keywords..

c. **Off-Page Optimization:** Create trustworthy backlinks from other authoritative websites to increase the website's reputation and trustworthiness.

d. **Technical SEO:** Ensure that the website has a solid technical foundation, which includes a proper site structure, mobile friendliness, rapid loading times, and secure connections.

e. **User Experience:** Improving the website's user experience, since search engines analyze user interaction data when ranking sites.

10 tried-and-true affiliate SEO strategies to increase traffic and revenue

While some online company SEO methods come and go, others endure. Let's go over 10 reliable affiliate SEO strategies that can boost your website traffic and revenue.

a. Select a keyword-rich domain name.

Before you construct your affiliate website, the struggle for rankings and profits begins. Before you publish a single word, you may acquire an SEO advantage over your competition by selecting a keyword-heavy domain name. Here are some pointers to help you choose the perfect domain name:

- **Keyword-rich, not keyword-deficient**: Make sure your domain name contains a traffic-attracting niche keyword. While you should strive to include your major keyword into your domain name, don't overdo it or you'll wind up with a silly, unnatural sounding name.

- **Not too lengthy, not too short**: Even if your name has an amazing keyword, consumers will have difficulty remembering it if it is winding. Create a brief and catchy name.

- **Simple, not complicated**: The last thing you want is for frantic individuals to spend their time attempting to figure out what your website's name means. To obtain more hits, create a basic, easy-to-spell name.

- **Not forgettable, but memorable**: Your domain name should be memorable. People will visit your website more often if the name is keyword-rich and memorable. So get a domain name that is memorable rather than generic.

Above all, if possible, get a dotcom extension. Because "dot com" is the most common top-level domain (TLD) name, prospective consumers anticipate it, and it provides a more familiar experience than going through to an unfamiliar extension. "marriage counsellor" is an excellent example of a good domain name since it is simple and memorable.

b.   Carry out outreach network-building initiatives.

Your link-worthy content assets will be useless if no one connects to them. This is where outreach connection building comes into play. Network building entails reaching out to website owners whose material your content assets may supplement. You request that they include your content resource as a value-added to their article. This is something that a freelance SEO or someone on your staff can readily do.

For the finest outreach link building outcomes, use these steps:

i.   **Make social networking a part of your daily routine**: Cold outreach is ineffective and has low conversion rates. Someone who knows you is more likely to reply favorably to your request. That is why you must publicize your name and grow relationship with individuals in your field before you need them.

ii.   **Concentrate on relatons rather than links**: Don't get too caught up in links. Instead, focus on relations since they provide you with ties and more -- partnerships, introductions to crucial niche players, and so on.

iii. **Make certain that you have super-duper link assets**: One major assumption underpins outreach link building: your content is amazing. You will not succeed unless you have outstanding content to connect to. Nobody wants to be linked to garbage.

iv.   **Offer something in exchange**: Increase your chances of success by providing something in return to the prospect. If applicable, you might offer a link exchange.

Perhaps you can provide them with free access to your useful tool or one of your contents.

c. Pay attention to keywords with high purchasing intent.

Not all keywords are created equal. It takes numerous steps and touches for a prospect to become a customer. As a result, keywords target various phases of the marketing funnel.

- Top of the funnel (TOFU) keywords

- Middle of the funnel (MOFU) keywords

- Bottom of the funnel (BOFU) keywords

Commercial intent keywords at the bottom of the funnel are used by individuals who are eager to purchase right now. You don't need to nurture these leads since they want to purchase your stuff right away. They just want a related product, therefore they hit the purchase button. These keywords contain the following popular search keywords:

Product-related keywords

- Best + product name e.g. best computer

- Product name searches e.g. HP computer

- Product categories, e.g. men's shorts, computer accessories, or laundry detergents.

- Top + product

Buy now searches

- Buy + product

- Product + Deal(s) e.g. computer deals

- Discount

- Coupons

- Cheap

Near me searches

Some local purchasers have an urgent requirement that cannot be postponed. They want to acquire a product or service right away as long as it is nearby—this is what near me searches are all about. They are most effective in local affiliate marketing.

Searches for "near me" look like this:

- Product + near me e.g. "pizza near me"
- Service + near me e.g. "barber near me"

d. Create long-form content guides that are linkable.

A Google search is the starting point for up to 59% of in-store and online transactions. So, if you publish quality content that incorporates keywords that people use to search for the things you're marketing, you'll be in good shape. Writing an in-depth review of the product you're marketing is a solid method to get your content (with affiliate links) to appear in search engines like Google, Bing, and Yahoo.

When you use the power of SEO, the effects are continuous. You earn money without having to do anything.

Here are some pointers to help you nail your review piece:

- Benefits are more important than features since features are lifeless components of a product. You must, indeed, touch them. However, for the greatest results, concentrate on how these characteristics will benefit your audience.
  Sell the sizzle rather than the steak. You'll earn more money and interact with more people.

- Be fair and impartial; your review should not be biased. Don't shout the product's virtues all the time. Discuss its flaws as well, so that your work is honest.

- Studies suggest that posts that rank on the main page are 2000k+ words lengthy. Investigate the product thoroughly to improve your chances of ranking. Make sure you address any and all questions concerning the product that consumers may have

e. Insert affiliate links into high-traffic pages.

You don't have to start from scratch with your affiliate SEO marketing since you can utilize current content assets. In three easy steps, here's how to accomplish it:

- **Check out your analytics dashboard.**

The first step is to determine your best-performing pages. To do so, log in to your Google Analytics account, Google Search Console, or chosen analytics tool and choose the most popular sites.

Use tools such as Google Search Console to determine your best-performing pages

- **Look for mentions of organic keywords.**

It's time to improve your top pages once you've chosen them. Open the relevant posts and look for your affiliate keywords in the article. When you've found a match, connect to your affiliate offerings.

- **Make changes to the page to suit affiliate keywords.**

While the preceding stage will uncover numerous keyword chances, it will not reveal all of them. You must put forth some effort to locate alternative options. Simply seek for an appropriate context in the content and modify brief sections before inserting the keywords.

f.   **Make a useful tool that others will appreciate.**

In certain categories, such as Software as a Service (SaaS), creating a helpful product is a simple but effective approach to bring significant traffic to your affiliate site. Everything comes down to four points:

- **Determine the appropriate problem to solve.**

First, identify a problem that your target customers have. For long-term sustainability, ensure that the issue is not transient. You may poll your target audience to identify and verify your decision.   For   example,   this   paycheck   calculator (https://www.paycheckcity.com/calculator/salary) is a very lightweight web application that receives a lot of traffic.

- **Create the appropriate tool to tackle the situation.**

Once you've found your target audience's itch, design a tool to scratch it. If you lack the necessary skills, outsource the task if you are confident in the software's potential.

- **Promote the tool to get the first round of traffic and visibility.**

Having a nice tools that nobody knows about will not benefit you. In the beginning, market your tool as much as possible so that people are aware of it. This will increase its SEO visitors. Once the product has gained popularity, word-of-mouth marketing will kick in as people naturally talk about your solution.

- **Determine the best product**

It is not sufficient to have a useful tool. You must also find the proper product(s) that precisely compliment your tool. This provides improved conversion and closure rates since your product is relevant to the tool's users' interests. The Keto Calculator from Perfect Keto (perfectketo.com) is a great illustration of this method. The remarkable figures suggest that the company struck a nerve:

a. 3.37k backlinks;

b. 3.3k organic keywords;

c. 16.5k organic traffic;

d. 16.8k traffic value.

g.   Make the most of the potential of pain-point SEO.

Pain is an excellent motivator. Especially if it's a product-related issue that people want to remedy right now. In case you're unfamiliar, pain point SEO is a technique that favors low volume, high-intent keywords above the standard high-volume keywords that everyone strives for. The assumption is that although high-intent keywords have lower volumes, they convert better because they address issues that are more closely related to the transaction. Here are five content kinds that work well for pain-point SEO.

- **Pricing products**

In this form of content, you talk about the price of the product or service you're marketing. Show the reader why the product is worthwhile. Alternatively, you may discuss rival products and add your affiliate products as a less expensive or more valuable choice.

g.   Comparison posts

This strategy entails comparing your affiliate products to the top products in your niche. Remember to be impartial throughout rather than just screaming your affiliate products' praises since you are looking for clicks.

- **"Alternatives to" posts**

This content form assists searchers in locating the best substitute for a popular product or service. All you have to do is choose the best products in your niche and then pitch your affiliate products as suitable substitutes. An example is HubSpot alternatives blog from https://www.nutshell.com/blog/best-hubspot-alternatives.

- **Use case posts**

You explain the common circumstances in which your affiliate products may be utilized in the use case content structure. Describe the issue (and solution) in detail so that readers may easily relate with it. When readers believe you understand their plight, they are more inclined to take you up on your offers.

Here's an example of a case study article on how to attract your prospects' attention (https://www.nutshell.com/blog/creative-sales-case-studies-to-steal-your-prospects-attention).

- **Best Products Posts**

Searchers are always on the lookout for the greatest products on the market. Best products fulfill this customer aim by giving a convenient list of the best products in a certain category. Simply insert the items you are selling into the list in the context of affiliate marketing. Here are a few such examples:

- A virtual event software post from the Nutshell.com (https://www.nutshell.com/blog/best-virtual-event-software-platforms).
- The best screencasting software post by Colinshipp.com (https://colinshipp.com/best-screencasting-software/)

h. **Make your content voice search friendly.**

Voice search is not going away. Currently, voice searches account for 50% of all searches (https://review42.com/voice-search-stats/). So, if you don't optimize your affiliate website for voice search, you'll be wasting money and falling behind your competition. Here are some points on making your contents voice searchable:

- **Write in a conversational tone rather than a formal one.**

Voice search is simply a discussion between a human and an intelligent computer. Use a casual approach in your content to attract voice search crawlers. You won't obtain results if you employ a stiff formal style since Voice Search Assistants are designed for natural voice requests, not keyword-stuffed text.

- **Incorporate a lot of questions into your text.**

Most voice inquiries are phrased as questions by searchers, for example. Where can I find the greatest Mediterranean restaurant near me? Incorporate queries into your content to increase your chances of appearing in voice searches.

Create a frequently asked questions (FAQ) website for your best products in addition to utilizing queries in blog articles.

- **Increase the number of long-tail keywords in your article.**

Voice search strings are up to five words longer than standard text-based searches. Optimize your sites for voice search by include numerous synonyms for your primary keywords in your content. To assist you come up with Latent Semantic Indexing (LSI) keywords, use a tool like Amazon Keyword Tool (https://www.keywordtooldominator.com/k/amazon-keyword-tool).

i. **Adopt a long-form content approach.**

We have discussed the effectiveness of long-form content as a link magnet. Long-form content is not only excellent for link acquisition, but it is also excellent for voice search engine attractiveness. Why is this the case? It's because when you write in detail about a subject, you naturally incorporate a lot of long-tail keywords.

j. Guest posts on prominent niche websites

Guest articles are a tried and true strategy of gaining links and visitors. Because it is now a popular mainstream practice, it is frequently overused or performed poorly. If you're going to use guest blogging in your affiliate marketing, you need to perfect it.

k. Pitch completely unique material.

Rehearsed pitches inundate editors' inboxes. They quickly reject such proposals since the offered content would not bring anything fresh to the discourse. The good news is that editors favor unique proposals that provide value to their audience. Before pitching a concept to an editor, consider if it will actually provide value to their audience.

l. Only guest write on relevant niche sites.

Don't chase guest posts just for the sake of checking it off your affiliate marketing to-do list. Pick your targets with the utmost care if you want to see tangible ROI from your guest posting campaigns. Choose widely popular high traffic (and domain authority) sites frequented by your ideal potential customers.

m. In the body of the guest post, provide a link to your material.

In the body of the guest post, provide a link to your material. If feasible, provide a link to your material in the body of the guest post. Most editors don't object if you link to a resource that adds value to the post. However, if the stuff you link to isn't contextually relevant, don't push it. Editors can notice forced unrelated links a mile away and delete them immediately.

n. Make the most of author bio linking possibilities.

While editors are stringent about links in the body of guest contributions, they let the author bio run wild. As a result, take advantage of this wonderful chance to link to the sites you're advertising.

o. Direct visitors to a certain landing page.

Using warm guest post traffic to drive to a homepage is a significant mistake. Most homepages are cluttered with advertisements. For improved conversions, direct that traffic to a distraction-free landing page and provide special tailor-made offers to your visitors.

p. Concentrate on long-tail keywords.

There is a frenzied rush for extremely competitive, high volume keywords in affiliate marketing circles. Everyone believes that is where the money is. Unfortunately, it is a misconception. Yes, you should concentrate on high-volume keywords.

However, including long-tail keywords into the mix will benefit you. Here are three reasons why you should use long-tail keywords into your affiliate SEO strategy:

- **Lower traffic equals greater conversions.**

Head keywords get a lot of traffic, but they don't convert very effectively. Long-tail keywords get less traffic but convert far better than head keywords since the traffic is more focused.

- **Higher conversions with more detailed copy**

Head keywords are succinct and have a wide appeal. Long-tail keywords are lengthier and enable users to be more particular about their requirements. This results in larger conversions, for example, tomatoes vs best fertilizer for tomatoes. According to Ahrefs research, 69.7% of search searches include four words or more, therefore lengthy tails give a fantastic possibility for development.

- **Less competition means quicker results.**

Because everyone is chasing head keywords, targeting long-tails will give you a better chance of success. They are juicy easy prospects since the keyword difficulty scores are quite low, allowing you to rank for them quickly. Ranking for high-volume keywords, on the other hand, takes a long time since competition is fierce.

Leveraging Social Media Platforms

Social media involvement is critical to affiliate marketing success. With the growing popularity of social media platforms, companies have realized the enormous potential that these platforms have for promoting their goods or services. Businesses may easily enhance brand recognition, attract traffic to their websites, and eventually raise sales by connecting with their target audience on social media.

Social networking sites provide affiliate marketers a unique chance to engage with their audience on a more personal level. Affiliate marketers may attract the attention of their followers and develop a devoted community by using engaging material such as videos, photos, and intriguing stories. Affiliate marketers may build trust and credibility by connecting with their audience via comments, likes, and shares, making it more probable for their followers to make a purchase.

Social media platforms

Affiliate marketers may use a variety of social media sites to promote their goods or services. Each platform has its own set of tools and targeting choices that affiliates may use to efficiently reach their target audience.

Affiliate marketers may use a variety of social media sites to promote their goods or services

a.   Facebook

Facebook is without a doubt one of the most popular social media networks, with over 2.8 billion monthly active members. Facebook advertising alternatives include targeted advertisements, sponsored posts, and Facebook Groups. Affiliates may leverage Facebook's rich user data to reach their target audience.

Almost everyone has a Facebook account. This is not a hyperbolic statement. People ranging in age from 13 to 65+ use Facebook on a regular basis. Don't be shocked if you come across accounts for dogs and cats as well! Facebook is widely utilized across the globe, with over 2.37 billion monthly active users.

It's pasttime to enhance your affiliate marketing methods in order to reach such a large audience.

- **Create a Facebook Page**

While you are performing affiliate marketing, placing links on your personal timeline may seem to your friends as spamming. Create a Facebook page instead. A page allows you to effortlessly publish content while also providing a complete review of your post-performance.

The catch is that you must develop and distribute quality content. Aside from providing constant content, it is also important to maintain engagement with your audience. Be active in comments and direct messages with the intention of assisting others, and you will inevitably enjoy the rewards of gaining more page followers.

To attract the correct target audience, you must first decide on a specialty before creating a page. You don't want your efforts to go awry. After you've decided on a topic, you may begin placing affiliate links on your page without seeming overly commercial.

- **Create or join a Facebook Group**

When compared to pages, groups have a better engagement rate. You may effortlessly communicate with the group members and give relevant information in your field. They will trust the products or services that you advocate after you have established your worth among the group members.

This results in a number of link hits, and there you have it - your affiliate marketing commission!

- **Ads on Facebook**

If you have a page where you upload affiliate marketing content, the key to success is to reach more and more individuals who are in the correct demographic. This is possible using Facebook Ads. Facebook offers highly targeted ad campaigns that may increase the reach and visibility of your posts. You may run the ad for the demographic, gender, age, and behavior pattern that you are looking for in your audience after you have a clear understanding of who your target audience is.

Using this Facebook advertisements checklist, ensure that you are optimizing the links you are posting. Affiliate links are readily identified and have a fishy feel to them. Nobody would click on links that do not seem to be genuine.

One way is to use internet link shortening tools and websites to shorten the URL. Some instance of link shortening services include:

- bitly
- tinyurl.com
- ow.ly
- buff.ly

b. **Instagram:**

Instagram is a popular medium for affiliate marketing because of its visually attractive and well selected content. Affiliates may use features like shoppable posts and Instagram Reels to promote engagement and sales by creating visually appealing posts and stories. Instagram is one of the most popular social networking program among Millenials and Gen-Z, with over 1 billion active monthly users and 500 million daily users.

Instagram is behind Facebook in terms of engagement, with 71% of users under the age of 35. In 2018, SimilarWeb assessed the average amount of time individuals spend on Instagram, which was 53 minutes per day. Affiliate marketers should take use of Instagram's potential as a social media platform to post product links.

But first, you must be an influencer in the area of the things you are recommending. This will guarantee that your fans have faith in you. Having more Instagram followers who actively interact is the key to obtaining more link clicks.

Also, make sure you have an Instagram Business Profile so you can monitor your audience and post performance.

- **Link in Bio**

Unlike Facebook, Instagram does not support direct link sharing. Instead, provide the affiliate link in your bio. You must edit your Bio every time you publish an affiliate marketing piece. A relevant and attractive image, followed by a clear description of the product in the text, is sufficient to notify your followers about the products.

Tell your followers to purchase the product by clicking the link in your profile. When it comes to Reach, Instagram hashtags work like a charm. You may reach those who aren't following you but are interested in the items you're marketing by using hashtags relating to the products and companies you're pushing.

And if these prospects appreciate the stuff you're providing, you've gained new fans!

- **Tools for selling directly via posts**

Many market solutions may be combined with your Instagram account to allow redirection to the website of the product with which you are associated. Curalate's Like2Buy tool is useful for making your photos and movies clickable. When your followers click on the post, this feature adds a link to your profile. They are then taken to the gallery to shop.

- **Instagram Stories**

You may publish your product affiliation link in your Instagram story's Swipe up. However, this is only achievable if you have more than 10,000 followers. You may connect your narrative picture to the product website using product creatives and short descriptions.

Stories are an excellent way to spice up your Instagram feed, engage your followers, and get new ones. If you don't have 10,000 followers, you may utilize link-shortening tools to make your affiliation link easier to memorize and write. People watch Instagram stories on a regular basis, and you have the perfect area to promote your link!

- **Instagram Post Promotions**

Paid Instagram advertisements are an excellent approach to reach a prospective audience that has not yet noticed you. You may sponsor Instagram posts by choosing the demographic and hobbies that you desire among your potential followers. It is also essential to export your Instagram statistics in order to evaluate the overall performance of your account.

Another strategy to boost your following is to hold competitions and freebies to encourage participation. You may attract followers and encourage them to promote your articles or account via their stories by giving discounts or gift codes.

c. Twitter

Because of Twitter's fast-paced and real-time nature, affiliate marketers may use it to post time-sensitive bargains and promotions. Affiliates may boost their exposure and generate traffic to their affiliate links by using relevant hashtags and interacting with their audience via retweets and replies. Twitter has approximately 330 million monthly active users, with 63% of this audience being between the ages of 35 and 65.

Instagram and Snapchat cater to the younger generation, whereas Twitter caters to the more older age group.

Affiliate marketers may use Twitter to post time-sensitive bargains and promotions

Being a microblogging site where you must summarize your message in 280 characters, you must be sharp and succinct. You already have information on the platform's users; now you must learn how to develop content. Be clever and inventive when it comes to Twitter affiliate marketing. Observing what your competitors are doing may assist you in developing the appropriate methods and material to share and promote. Twitter Tools may help you manage your followers, tweets, and retweets, which can help you optimize your profile. You may use the following tools:

- Circleboom (https://circleboom.com/)

- SocialPilot (https://www.socialpilot.co/)

- Audiense (https://www.audiense.com/)

Improve your Twitter bio

It's difficult to sum oneself up in 160 characters. But when it comes to crafting a Twitter bio, you simply have one option: nail it! Your bio should be brief and representative of who you are.

It must be consistent with your tweets and other Twitter engagements. Give it a voice by using your own. It is not a good idea to demonstrate that you are here to sell. However, including a link to your blog or website is also beneficial.

Again, the goal is to make it sophisticated and understated. Genuine interaction is required to be noticed. Interactions, regardless of platform, help you to be recognized. Retweet and comment on pertinent stuff. Participate in Twitter conversations to share your thoughts.

You will be adding value to your network's feed in this manner. You are also participating to twitter threads on your area of expertise and interest. And before long, you may find yourself as someone to look up to in your field.

You may also connect with influencers in your field. By cultivating connections with influencers, you not only pave the road for endorsements, but you can also expect a lot of word-of-mouth marketing to come your way.

Create content on a regular basis.

It is not just competition that drives you to create content every day; you must also keep yourself informed. That is why you must tweet on a regular basis. Make certain that you are publishing at the appropriate time.

Check out the ideal times to tweet on Twitter to get the most interaction. If you want to create visual content in bulk for all of these networks, you can utilize a tool like Venngage (venngage.com) to do it fast and easily. Furthermore, Twitter is a site where you may get ideal outcomes by using hashtags.

Use hashtags that are related to your content. Check the popular hashtags to see if they match what you're tweeting. Using hashtags assists you in organizing and sorting your information. It benefits folks who are interested in your material but have not yet found you.

Twitter Ads and Analytics

Marketers benefit greatly from analytics. You may monitor the effectiveness of your tweets as well as their popularity among your followers. This also helps in determining what your audience loves and dislikes based on the response you get on your tweets.

Another thing to remember about analytics is to make your tweets visually appealing. You may increase interaction on your tweets by using relevant images and videos. When it comes to Twitter advertisements, you may look at the many choices for running campaigns to enhance affiliate marketing.

Twitter Ads may be used to get new followers, generate leads, or promote affiliate marketing opportunities.

Gaining followers

You may promote your tweets in order to get more followers. In this case, Twitter displays your tweet to a specific audience that you may set from the backend based on demographics and behavior. After you've identified the campaign, create a captivating message and a CTA that leads to new followers.

Remember, you're conducting this campaign to get new followers, not to sell products. As a result, the CTA and messaging must be congruent with this purpose.

To interact with the audience

You're investing your time, money, and effort to achieve a goal, right? After all, generating conversions is the primary purpose of advertising your tweets. This form of Twitter campaign assists you in directing your followers to the next step, which is to visit your website.

Use a conversion tracking mechanism to keep track of the actions taken by your visitors. This might include subscribing to your email, placing product purchases, or changing the time and frequency of your sessions. Create a Universal Website Tag and post it on your websites to measure conversions for sophisticated business tracking on Twitter.

Pinterest

Pinterest affiliate marketing differs from the others mentioned above. It's all about making boards and pinning here. The first step for everyone new to the site is to establish boards.

These message boards must be in the same industry as the items you are supporting. Create boards related to affiliate marketing in kitchen items or home décor, for example. Create eight to ten similar boards using various items.

Here are a few examples:

- Healthcare Advice
- Book Recommendation
- Home Decor
- Travel Destinations
- Pets, and so forth.

Each board should include a description. Finally, provide a link to your related products that are relevant to the board. Add pins to the boards once they have been created.

It is difficult to add pins, which is why I propose utilizing a program that will assist you in quickly inserting pins. I've mentioned a few tools that may help you manage your Pinterest account below;

- Buffer (https://buffer.com/)
- Tailwind (https://www.tailwindapp.com/)
- ViralWoot (https://viralwoot.com/)
- Loop88 (https://www.loop88.com/)

Optimize your Pinterest account

After you've made boards and posted pins to them, you can concentrate on obtaining followers who are interested in the stuff you've pinned. You may schedule pins on your boards on a weekly basis using the tools listed above. Schedule posts at a time when you can gain the most interaction.

This participation might take the shape of repins, website clicks, or product orders. Social media scheduling also makes managing many social accounts simpler. Also, if you want to get noticed on Pinterest, repin the stuff provided by influencers. You may participate in group boards to get exposure to a wide range of information.

Unlike other social media networks, Pinterest Ads are seldom necessary. To acquire momentum on your Pinterest account, you might instead invest in solutions that help automate your Pinterest interactions.

Snapchat

Snapchat is a relatively newcomer to the social media scene. But be warned: it's not for the faint of heart. You may be wondering how this ephemeral image and video sharing network will benefit you as an affiliate marketer.

However, you may be in the dark there. Allow me to clear the air and explain how Snapchat may be used to communicate with customers aged 18-24, the platform's most active users. It may be tough to become known on Snapchat, but with the right baby steps, you can get there.

Snapchat post contains no hashtags or reposts. So the only method to get followers is to follow individuals and communicate with them via snaps.

How can Snapchat assist you with affiliate marketing?

- Share product launch teasers to raise curiosity and excite your audience's interest.
- Make offerings that will pique your followers' interest. Because the photographs and videos are only available for 24 hours, take advantage of this opportunity.

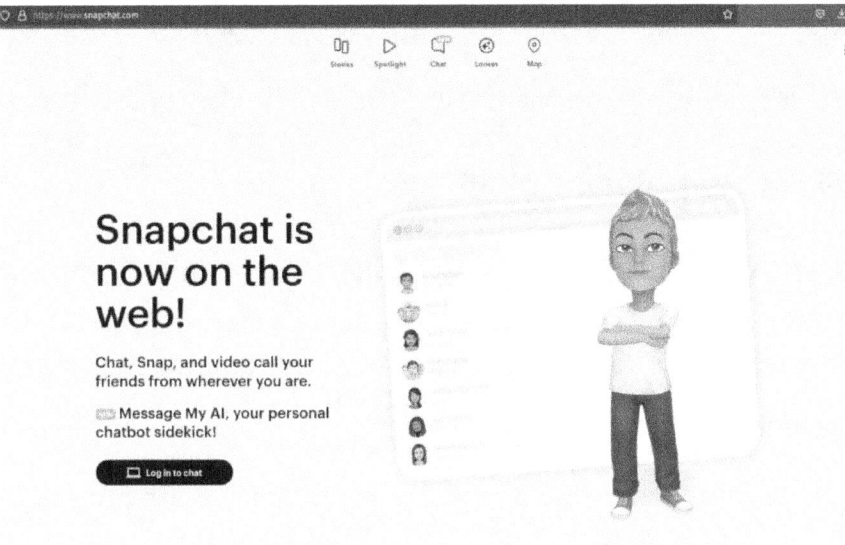

Customers aged 18-24 are the Snapchat's most active users.

- Give content access to a select set of people who are loyal to you. Make them feel unique by giving them reward points for purchases or exclusive offers.

- Use the Snapchat Live function to interact with your followers while attending trade shows or product launch events, for example.

- Hold competitions and freebies to engage your fans.

You may always try with other things. You will learn what works best for you on Snapchat with the audience at hand using the trial and error technique.

YouTube

YouTube, as a video-sharing network, provides affiliates with a unique chance to develop compelling and instructive content. Affiliates may make product reviews, tutorials, or unboxing videos and add affiliate links in the video description or via YouTube's partner program. As an affiliate marketer, your objective is to get individuals to buy things from you in exchange for a commission.

YouTube is an excellent venue for doing so. YouTube is now the world's second-most popular social media network, and by 2025, the channel is expected to have about one billion subscribers worldwide. Viewers visit their favorite YouTube channels to acquire skills, investigate information, and make purchase choices, as well as to enjoy themselves.

YouTube's Advantages for Affiliate Marketing

When it comes to YouTube affiliate marketing, affiliates have various advantages:

- Because videos are the most often shared type of content, they may help you generate highly engaged audiences.

- Using videos to monetise your channel with affiliate marketing is a great method to make money passively.

- Optimizing your videos for SEO may enhance your presence on search engine results pages (SERPs) and visitors.

- When compared to typical content, compelling YouTube product videos have the potential for greater conversion rates for an affiliate link.

- It may assist in tapping a lucrative market. When making a shopping choice, 68% of consumers viewed a YouTube video. Affiliate links connect YouTube visitors to products featured in content such as how-to videos.

How can I get started with affiliate marketing on YouTube?

Simply join affiliate programs via your favorite businesses and insert affiliate links in your YouTube video descriptions to get started as an affiliate marketer on YouTube. You get compensated when your audience is inspired to buy as a result of your video. With the YouTube Shopping affiliate network, you may unlock new revenue opportunities as your company grows. To be invited to join in this YouTube affiliate marketing program, you must first complete the following steps:

Achieving a subscription base of at least 20,000 people.

a. Participating in the YouTube Partner Program (YPP), which has lower subscriber requirements than the affiliate program.

b. Verifying your location in the United States.

c. Reviewing and adhering to YouTube's Community Guidelines, which establish the platform's content standards.

d. Going through a channel audit to ensure compliance with YouTube's monetization standards.

How to Participate

You can sign up in YouTube Studio once you've qualified for the program.

a. Enter your YouTube Studio username and password.

b. Select Earn from the left menu.

c. Click Join Now under Programs.

d. Study and accept the Terms of Service for the YouTube Affiliate Program.

e. You're in! You may begin tagging products in your article. Ensure that you follow the tagging standards.

Here are some types of videos that can help you become an affiliate marketer:

How-To Videos

How-To videos are instructional videos in which YouTubers explain or teach how to do a certain activity. These videos are well-liked by viewers because they are both instructive and entertaining. In these videos, you may explain anything that is difficult for your target audience to utilize or comprehend in a meaningful way.

As a result, these 'How-To' videos may cover anything from solving mathematical problems to using editing tools.

Product Review Videos

You must explain why a certain product is excellent or poor and whether your audience should purchase it or not in product review videos. One of the most well-known instances of product reviews on YouTube is smartphone review videos. Many individuals evaluate vehicles, books, cosmetic items, video games, and movies, among other things.

Review videos, more than any other sort of video material, may help you get an affiliate marketing contract more faster.

One of the most well-known instances of product reviews on YouTube is smartphone review videos.

'Best Of' Videos

While navigating through your YouTube site, you may come across videos that discuss the "Top 10" or "Best of" whatever. These videos are quite simple to make. All you have to do is develop a list of the products you want to promote and speak about them.

The general guideline in these "list" videos is to start with your least favorite thing and work your way up to your favorite. In the description, you may include affiliate links to all of the products featured in your video.

Unboxing Videos

The name is self-explanatory. Unboxing is the process of opening a freshly purchased product in front of a camera and recording your initial impressions of it. While it may seem unusual to watch a stranger unbox and discuss a product, millions of consumers find such material intriguing. Perhaps it stems from seeing someone show their excitement at obtaining the desired product and casually discuss it. For a change, this is also where customers see a product put outside of its planned marketing effort.

Vlogs

You may produce vlogs on YouTube if you are a travel enthusiast or someone who enjoys filming videos on a regular basis. Although creating vlogs is a time-consuming procedure, the rewards are enormous. Vlogs demand excellent video editing abilities.

You may include affiliate links for all of the equipment you used for vlogging or traveling (if it's a trip vlog) in the description box. If you believe you can engage people with vlogs, grab your phone and start filming.

Pro YouTube Tips for Success

You will need a large audience to benefit from a YouTube affiliate marketing arrangement. Assume you get one million views on a video. At least 5 to 10% of the viewers are likely to click on the affiliate link, increasing your chances of generating purchases.

As a result, having more views on your videos might result in more earnings. You must create compelling videos in order to attract more views and subscribers. Here are some tips to get you started:

Pay attention to audio quality.

Nobody will watch a video in which what you are saying is not properly heard. As a result, before posting a video, double-check the audio clarity. Try to capture videos in a confined, soundproof environment, or at the very least, reduce any distracting background sounds.

Make a suitable script.

Having a script will help you stay on topic in your videos. It would help you avoid uncomfortable silences and pauses. This practice will be appreciated by your audience. Even if you're recording vlogs, having some ideas for what you'll say and do might help.

Edit videos

Nobody can do everything perfectly in one take. Remove any elements that offer no value to your video. Give your viewers a final edit that is worth their time.

Create YouTube Shorts

Making compelling videos is important, but don't overlook the trend of YouTube Shorts. Creators may use YouTube shorts to make TikTok-style films of 60 seconds or fewer that attract viewers' attention immediately owing to their short runtime and compelling content. Shorts are intended to capitalize on YouTubers' existing audience's short attention span by providing bite-sized material that can quickly reach the masses.

This was all that you needed to know before starting affiliate marketing on YouTube. Keep in mind that the more affiliate links you promote, the more money you'll earn. Make your videos as entertaining as possible to increase your sales.

You may also partner with other well-known YouTubers to expand your reach. However, bear in mind that marketing substandard products and services might give your viewers the incorrect impression. As a result, don't market products only to make money.

YouTube affiliate marketing is particularly advantageous for businesses since the return on investment is far higher than that of most other marketing channels.

LinkedIn

LinkedIn is a professional networking site that might be especially beneficial for affiliates targeting a business-to-business audience. Affiliates may provide industry insights, thought leadership pieces, and relevant material to position themselves as subject matter experts and create leads. LinkedIn affiliate marketing is a kind of performance-based marketing that mainly targets businesses and utilizes LinkedIn as a key marketing platform.

Affiliate marketing on LinkedIn may take numerous forms, from blogging to personal sales. Affiliate marketing on LinkedIn isn't very popular since most people attempt to sell their own items rather than affiliate products. However, this is more of an untapped potential than an impediment.

LinkedIn has an engaged audience and several methods to get users to click on affiliate links - a winning mix for a partner. One of the biggest and most crucial benefits of affiliate marketing on LinkedIn, and what makes it so profitable, is its audience. LinkedIn is a social network for discussing career triumphs and networking with colleagues, not for publishing holiday images.

LinkedIn boasts 65 million decision makers – CEOs, CMOs, and others in positions that enable them to decide whether or not to partner with you. This implies that salesmen won't have to go through the company to locate someone ready to look at their offer. They may speak with them directly.

Will having access to such a vast number of individuals aid your marketing efforts? It very well may, since 45% of marketers say LinkedIn is essential for lead creation. Not only do decision-makers utilize LinkedIn, but they also want to network on the site. LinkedIn does have certain disadvantages. The first is almost entirely limited to B2B goods and services.

This isn't a major disadvantage, but it will hinder you from using this social networking site if you have a particular affiliate product to market. If you're determined to promote on LinkedIn, all you need to do is select a suitable affiliate deal to work with. Another issue that may make affiliate marketing on LinkedIn difficult is the high cost of in-platform advertisements.

If you want to increase the number of people who see your content, it might cost you up to $6 per 1000 impressions. That is more expensive than other social networks, but having more individuals eager to locate commercial opportunities makes up for it.

How to Make the Most of LinkedIn for Affiliate Marketing

One of the most significant benefits of LinkedIn for marketing is its versatility. Let's look at three tactics for affiliate marketing on LinkedIn that will provide the finest results.

Begin talks

Talking business to people on social media is a terrific way to get started with affiliate marketing on the network. You may initiate discussions with folks who are either directly interested in the affiliate product you're marketing or may be interested in it. That may be accomplished by speaking with them directly if they are in your network, or by sending them an InMail message for $0.80 each message.

This helps you to develop a more personal connection with the leads, but it also takes a lot longer to close a transaction. With InMail, this essentially becomes email marketing and can be automated in the same way that normal email marketing can. However, because of the high price per message, you must have a very solid payment plan on the affiliate marketing offer in order for it to be lucrative.

Make a blog.

Increasing your LinkedIn following might be difficult, but it is worthwhile. There are several successful blogs on the site, with the majority of them concentrating on assisting other companies and exchanging experiences. Some blogs operate as business public relations tools. Some blogs concentrate on garnering publicity for either a business or an individual, aiming to establish a personal brand.

This is the kind of blog that an affiliate marketer might run. Because the information you end up with is significantly shorter, it may seem like running a blog requires much less labor than publishing full-length articles on the site. But that is not the case; blogging requires significant labor as well, if not for the actual writing of the piece, then for research and analytics.

To raise the number of followers and viewership so that affiliate items can catch up, do the following.

a. Know your target audience and what they're searching for.

b. Use LinkedIn's Content Suggest function to hunt for topics to cover.

c. Provide valuable information based on statistics, expertise, and insights.

d. Utilize hashtags

e. Take part in industry conversations on other blogs and organizations.

f. Use matched audiences advertisements to target those who are already interested in the subject.

g. Examine the reach and change in followers of each post to see what works best.

Product articles

LinkedIn Pulse enables content to appear in search results. You may get your content to the top 10 if your website is deemed as highly authoritative by search engines. The amount of followers has no bearing on how effective the post will be on SERP; only the content of the post does.

If you want to experiment with affiliate marketing on LinkedIn Pulse, do it in the same way you would with marketing on your own website. Concentrate on themes that are related to your affiliate product. Keyword difficulty will be minimal since LinkedIn outperforms any website you might construct in terms of SEO.

Once you've decided on a few themes to discuss, do keyword research and utilize the results to generate excellent content. With a little off-site SEO effort, your new piece will quickly rank high in SERPs, providing you with a consistent stream of readers. You may next concentrate on refining the CTA of the affiliate link to improve conversions.

How do I choose an affiliate marketing program on LinkedIn?

Now that you know LinkedIn is a good match for you, let's look at the programs available to you. Here's how to choose an affiliate program for your LinkedIn profile.

Look for a B2B company that has an affiliate program.

B2C items are used in many affiliate marketing networks. That is not the case at LinkedIn. You'll need a B2B company that offers services to individuals who prefer LinkedIn - most likely a digital company.

You may locate an affiliate program by examining expert resources or just searching Google. Most affiliate programs want visibility, therefore they will push their way into articles that score high on SERPs. You may also check with numerous prominent organizations that you know or have previously dealt with; chances are, they offer an affiliate program.

Find a few of firms that seem to be a good match in terms of the industry they're in and investigate them further.

Find favorable payment arrangements.

You're mostly interested in the affiliate program's payout structure and cookie duration. Some programs pay a flat fee per qualifying lead or 1000 views, while others give a revenue split. Coupler.io, for example, has a revenue sharing arrangement. Affiliate partners get a 50% discount on their first purchase and a 20% discount on renewals.

That is, if the customer continues with the firm, you may generate money without doing anything. That would amount to $150-$500 each lead's lifespan on average. However, B2B customers do not make choices on the moment. That is why you should investigate how cookies function with the firm you choose.

In typically, a cookie is allocated to a lead after their first visit via the affiliate link and lasts for 30 days. This means you'll be paid if they buy a Coupler.io subscription within 30 days of visiting the website via your affiliate link.

Examine their feedback.

The final and most significant step is to look into the company's reviews. Make sure it's a well-known group that has been running for a long and has received positive feedback. Otherwise, you risk becoming a part of a massive hoax and paying for it with your own reputation.

Is LinkedIn a good place to promote affiliate products?

In terms of affiliate marketing, LinkedIn is a relatively underutilized resource. Despite the fact that the platform may be used to earn income in a variety of ways, it is not commonly utilized. Find a good affiliate program that addresses B2B difficulties for customers that use LinkedIn. Experiment with the format of the information you post, and you could discover that it turns out to be a gold mine for you.

Where can I discover things to promote on LinkedIn?

LinkedIn is an excellent resource for affiliate marketers looking for items to promote. You may search for particular goods or explore popular categories to discover something that piques your interest. To locate items to promote on LinkedIn, start by searching for the product type you're looking for.

For example, if you want to market products in the health and fitness niche, you may seek for "health and fitness products." Once you've identified a few possible products to promote, visit the company's LinkedIn profile. Check to see if they have any special deals or discounts that you may publicize to your target audience.

Check out their reviews to see what other people have to say about the product. If you're still unsure about which product to promote, call out to your LinkedIn network to see if anybody has any suggestions. Once you've identified some decent goods to market, begin sharing them with your network to see how much interest you can create.

With a little work, you may quickly start producing sales and income from LinkedIn.

How to Make an Affiliate Marketing LinkedIn Profile

LinkedIn is particularly beneficial for affiliate marketing since it enables you to connect with other marketers and share ideas. Here are some pointers for developing a LinkedIn profile that can help you succeed in affiliate marketing:

a. Use titles that are keyword-rich and appropriately represent your abilities and expertise.

b. Create a compelling description that showcases your talents and outlines what you can offer prospective customers.

c. In your profile, provide links to your website and blog.

d. Join LinkedIn groups and forums to connect with other marketers.

You'll be well on your way to developing a successful LinkedIn profile for affiliate marketing if you follow these guidelines. Remember to keep it professional and avoid bombarding individuals with sales pitches!

How to Make the Most of LinkedIn Ads for Affiliate Marketing

Here are some pointers and ideas for promoting your affiliate items using LinkedIn ads:

a. **Use LinkedIn to reach out to your intended audience**: LinkedIn is a fantastic medium for reaching out to business professionals. You may tailor your advertising to the correct audience by using LinkedIn's targeting options, and you can also target by profession, occupation, company size, and other characteristics.

b. **Create a captivating advertising campaign**: People should click on your LinkedIn ad campaign if it is intriguing and exciting. Make sure your ad headline is appealing and your material is convincing.

c. **Make use of high-quality photos**: High-quality photographs are the greatest method to draw attention to your LinkedIn ad. Make sure your images are clear and professional.

By following these guidelines, you can design a successful LinkedIn ad campaign that will help you successfully sell your affiliate products. Experiment with various targeting choices and ad wording to determine what works best for your company. Remember to track your outcomes so you can continue to improve your efforts over time.

Advantages of Using LinkedIn for Affiliate Marketing

LinkedIn is not your average affiliate marketing website with a slew of affiliate links attempting to drive online purchases. Using this powerful technology provides several benefits in addition to earning money via affiliate marketing. LinkedIn may help entrepreneurs find new customers, reach a larger audience, create user trust, and expand their company.

Here's how you can use LinkedIn to boost your affiliate marketing efforts in particular.

a. LinkedIn affiliate marketing enables one to target more specialized and targeted audiences, which is effective in generating more leads and improving conversion rates while increasing user trust.

b. Because of the social network's enormous user base, businesses may easily identify affiliate marketers producing high-quality promotional content on numerous prominent marketing platforms.

c. You can use your LinkedIn connections to grow your email list, form collaborations, gain trust, and eventually generate more affiliate sales.

d. Marketers may join industry-specific LinkedIn groups to learn more about affiliate and email marketing methods from a diverse variety of experienced teams; such cooperation often leads to innovation and increased online sales.

e. With LinkedIn's powerful search features, effective affiliate marketers may more efficiently target particular affiliate program prospects.

f. LinkedIn's monitoring system assists affiliates in identifying excellent promotional content (blog articles on health and fitness, travel blogs, and so on) in their specialty. This way, you may improve your affiliate marketing plan, grow your email list, use popular marketing channels more effectively, and eventually earn more money with affiliate marketing.

Finally, conducting online affiliate marketing programs via LinkedIn is part of a holistic business plan and may be an excellent supplement to your email campaigns and promotional content publishing. Affiliate marketers and independent sellers may be certain that they are making the most of their affiliate marketing efforts.

Chapter 5: Crafting Compelling Content

"It's about you influencing more people by creating content that's easy to consume." –Frank Kern

Importance of Quality Content

Content marketing is a mission-critical growth approach for most organizations since it is one of the most successful means of increasing audience engagement, expanding your brand visibility, and generating sales. Let's go over content marketing in more detail, including the advantages of providing regular, high-quality content and how you quantify success. Content marketing is vital because it helps you create trust, develop connections, enhance conversions, and generate leads by answering your audience's queries.

Customers nowadays demand high-quality, consistent content from their favorite businesses.

Advantages of Content Marketing

a.   Your audience will stay longer.

Great content is a valuable asset. It has the potential to provide good experiences for your prospective customers and entice them to return for more. It's your key to attracting your audience's attention and maintaining a favorable brand image.

b. Your social media presence will improve.

It's one thing to grow your social media following across several platforms, but it's quite another to produce trending content. If your company isn't getting much traction despite having a large following, it's time to start using content marketing to your benefit. Quality content might assist your company in gaining popularity on social media.

Using HubSpot's analytics platform[1], you can monitor the success of your content marketing efforts.

c. Your audience will believe you.

Creating content allows your company to connect with its target audience. You may connect with clients and answer their inquiries. Your audience is more inclined to believe your advise and suggestions if you provide value without expecting anything in return.

Having your contents appear in the right location and at the right time with the appropriate audience can help your brand's reputation. Customers are more likely to develop a good relationship with your business if they see more high-quality content.

d. You will produce more and higher-quality leads.

Leads may also be generated via content marketing. When your audience consumes your material, they are more likely to make a subsequent purchase from you. Furthermore, calls-to-action (CTAs) included in your content might create fresh leads for your sales staff.

---

[1] https://www.hubspot.com/products/marketing/analytics

Having your contents appear in the right location and at the right time with the appropriate audience can help your brand's reputation.

So, how can content be used to create leads? Typically, you generate content to deliver relevant, free information to visitors. CTAs may be placed wherever in your content: inline, at the bottom of the article, in the hero, or even on the side panel.

The more satisfied a reader is with your content, the more likely they are to click your CTA and go to your landing page.

e.   Unique content may boost conversions.

Conversions are influenced by the content you publish. It allows your audience to interact with you and provides them with the knowledge they need to make informed purchases. If you're utilizing blog material to drive traffic, try employing unique visuals rather than stock photographs, since marketers indicate that the latter is the least successful in assisting them in meeting their objectives.

Furthermore, your material should always have a CTA and direct the reader on what to do next.

f.   SEO will increase the visibility of your company.

The more consistent and high-quality content you provide, the better your SEO efforts will be. For example, your content should assist your business in being visible online while also establishing trust and authority with your target audience. Furthermore, if you have a well-developed content strategy, such as the pillar/cluster model, your material should help you rank better in search engines.

g.   Excellent content may establish your company as an industry expert.

Creating high-quality content will also aid in the development of your online authority. If your company is seen as a reliable source of information, you are more likely to rank higher in search engines. Furthermore, if your customers see you as an industry expert, they are more likely to trust you.

Your content should display your competence in your subject while also answering the questions of your readers. Content marketing is critical in general. But how can you do it successfully? Assessing the quality of your material is one method to know. Content scoring is a particularly useful method of assessing quality.

There has never been a better moment to add content score analytics into your marketing campaign as more organizations boost their content marketing effort. You can use content scoring to assess and enhance your content marketing success while also providing exceptional value to your audience.

h.   You will create brand advocates.

Taking brand awareness a step further, all of the individuals who gushed about your content and linked all of those wonderful sentiments with your company are quite likely to become brand champions even before buying your goods. What am I saying? It's true that brand fans may be just as loyal and influence their friends' and family's purchasing choices when new customers realize that a company gives value to its present audience. Content marketing is one of the most effective methods for businesses to do this.

i.   Your marketing plan will be less expensive.

Blog content estimates vary from $150 per post to $3,000 for a freelance writer, but you could hire a full-time staff writer to develop content for you on a regular basis. When compared to sponsored commercials, video marketing, and conventional marketing, content always wins.

What exactly is content scoring?

The technique of measuring and quantifying the genuine potential of content by monitoring how individual content pieces perform in terms of generating and converting leads is known as content scoring. Content scoring, as an innovative content marketing measure, assists marketers in prioritizing just the assets that have a better likelihood of generating and converting leads.

Content scoring is a dependable and predictive approach of measuring the engagement potential of an individual piece of content before it is released, in addition to providing a scientific method of evaluation to authoring.

Improving your content's quality is critical to the success of any marketing initiatives.

The quality of your content is proportional to the profile of your audience. With a greater awareness of your customers' demands, you can provide more relevant information. However, enhancing your content takes time, and you must constantly evaluate and analyze your audience's reactions in order to learn and improve on the most important components.

How to Evaluate Your Content

Writers and content producers sometimes struggle to quantify what formula works best for their content and audience. By rating your content, you can objectify that process and utilize the same formula to generate equally effective content in the future. Here's how you can rate your content:

a. **Create scoring criteria**: To create an efficient content scoring system, you must first lay the groundwork using whichever engagement measure has the biggest influence on your content. For some, it may be page views, while for others, it could be social media shares.

b. **Make a campaign:** Create a campaign and include the successful content that satisfies your threshold after you've determined which measure is most important to you. For instance, if you determine that 1,000 page views is a high-performing metric, add all content pieces that satisfy that criterion.

c. **Keep an eye on the performance of your content:** Analyze the performance of each new piece of content you publish. Add content assets to the campaign when they reach your success criteria, such as 1,000 page views. Continue to add material in order to create a small sample size of high-performing content. Track the performance of this content with HubSpot Analytics.

d. **Examine what works:** Now that you've identified your high-performing content, you can dig further into what makes it tick. Although it is tough to measure, you may find trends in your content and duplicate them.

e. **Repeat as necessary:** Despite the fact that these patterns are always changing, this manual procedure is an efficient technique to assess your material and act on your discoveries in the future.

This may be a time-consuming procedure that just scratches the surface of a comprehensive content score system, but it is a rigorous and critical process to adopt.

Content scoring allows your business to establish a standard for itself, bringing you closer to understanding your customers' purchase stages and expectations. When you've identified the content formats that perform best for a given customer category, you can quickly reproduce your success.

What Exactly is Quality Content?

Definitions of what constitutes excellent content might change throughout time. Because Internet trends are frequently transient, the do's and don'ts of content today may not be the same in five or ten years. When keywords first became prominent, it was common practice to pack keywords into contents, which worked for a time.

Keyword stuffing, on the other hand, is now frowned upon. That being said, some content methods will almost certainly remain constant, since they form the cornerstone of what constitutes excellent content. So, what exactly is excellent content?

Keyword stuffing is now frowned upon.

Quality content is any material that adds value to the reader's life. In other words, rather than writing for search engines, you should write for your audience. It should be something new and intriguing for your viewers, not something you publish only to enhance your ranking on Google SERPs.

Yes, SEO and search engine rankings are vital, but if your content is designed just for that purpose, your viewers will notice, and they will lose interest. As a result, your material should be crafted for your customers while simultaneously considering SEO.

To do so, just put yourself in the shoes of your target audience and examine the following questions:

- Is it significant?
- Is it instructive or informative?

- Is it beneficial?

How To Create Quality Content That Suits Your Target Audience

Now let's get into the "how." How do you produce high-quality content? How can you create more engaging material for your readers?

- **Be Aware of Your Target Audience**

If you want to develop content that readers will like, you must first understand who they are and what is important to them. Take some time before you begin producing your content to investigate your target audience so that you can adapt your content to their individual interests and demands.

- **Be Aware of Your Competition**

In addition to studying your target audience, it is also beneficial to investigate what your competitors are doing. This will give you an indication of what content is hot and what you need to do to distinguish out from your competition or at the very least keep up with them. However, your "competition" includes customer concerns as well as competitor businesses.

If your content does not address these problems, you will lose customer relevance. To remain ahead of the competition, constantly address consumer issues and apathy to keep them motivated and fully involved.

a. **Be Informative and Entertaining**

Content that is helpful to the reader is both entertaining and educational. If your content achieves none of these things, it lacks significance and value and hence fails to keep your customer's attention.

But be careful not to stray too far in either way. Information that is just entertaining but not educational has no substance, while information that is solely informative but not engaging is boring. It all comes down to striking a balance between the two.

b. Think Outside the Box

While it is crucial to develop trending content, it is equally necessary to strive to break the mold and create something unique. Trendy material will keep you competitive, but original and creative content will help you stand out and put your business in the limelight.

c. Be True and Transparent

Customers nowadays are far more skeptical of the businesses with whom they choose to interact. In other words, flamboyant marketing strategies from the past are no longer effective. If you actually want to connect and capture your audience's attention, you must be honest and open with them.

Customers do not want companies that put on a show for them. They want companies that are prepared to be open and honest with them. Today, customers value honesty, sincerity, and openness much more than a clever advertisement.

Make sure your content is clear and doesn't have any hidden agendas that your viewers aren't aware of. If your content is merely a disguised sales pitch, your readers will see straight through it.

d. Know When to Post and When to Stop

When it comes to producing high-quality material, it's not just about quantity; it's also about timeliness. Even if your information is of high quality, it may not be as effective as you would want if it is not delivered on time. This is where content scheduling software comes in handy.

It may assist you in developing the best plan for when your content will be most successful. Keep in mind, however, that certain stuff is best uploaded straight away. Certain social media trends, for example, might fade and become old and stale in a matter of days, so if you want to capitalize on such trends, you must typically move quickly.

e. Consider the Short and Long Term

Content that provides topical value now is equally as vital as content that will provide relevant information in the future. Seasonal or time-sensitive content is referred to as topical content. It's content that capitalizes on trending subjects and items that are causing a stir. Evergreen content is ageless – it is material that can be used again and over because it is always relevant.

When developing high-quality content, it's critical to strike a balance between the two. Topical material will offer you instant hits, but evergreen content will bring you a constant stream of visitors over time.

f.   Testing and Measurement Results

Finally, in order to verify that your material gets the expected objectives, you must test and assess your efforts using data, whether you are running a campaign, for example, you do not want to wait until the end to determine whether it was successful or not, since this might result in lost time and money.

Instead, you should assess progress along the way so that you may make modifications as required. This way, you'll always know how well or poorly your work is being received. This helps you to solve problems as they arise, rather than waiting until the conclusion of a time period to see if your material was successful or not.

Writing Effective Product Reviews

Product reviews for affiliate marketing may promote sales for an affiliate product if they are effectively written. However, the goal of affiliate product evaluations is to develop trust among your audience as well as to increase sales. Only when your target audience values your product evaluations and other content will they be inclined to click on your affiliate links.

According to research, roughly 79% of buyers depend on and trust internet evaluations just as much as personal recommendations. So, if your review is dishonest or leads to a terrible bargain, you risk losing the consumer's confidence and goodwill for good. So, how can you guarantee that your product reviews both establish confidence and promote sales?

We'll go over all of this and more in our discussion on how to create the best product reviews for affiliate marketing. What are the many sorts of product reviews used in affiliate marketing? Before we go into how to create an exceptional product review for your affiliate site, you need be aware of the many types of product reviews available. A product review may be written in a variety of styles. It might be a short or lengthy blog entry on its own.

Product reviews for affiliate marketing may promote sales for an affiliate product if they are effectively written.

Product reviews that are brief

You might opt to create a quick product review for your affiliate marketing website. These reviews are not often written for a particular product. You may have come across websites that provide short evaluations of various affiliate items that are grouped together.

To provide additional depth, the quick assessment is often accompanied with a star rating or a number rating. Typically, an affiliate link to the product on the merchant site is included at the conclusion of the review. These evaluations are ideal for anybody who needs to make a fast buying choice at a glance.

They are adequate for less priced products/services that would be purchased without much deliberation.

Comprehensive Product Evaluations

These are significantly more in-depth and comprehensive assessments of affiliate items. A thorough review covers all elements of the product and attempts to address any queries that customers may have about it. A review like this, on the other hand, must be written really effectively in order for the reader to be persuaded to click on your affiliate link.

With a shorter review, readers are more likely to click on the affiliate link since they need more information about the items from the merchant site. However, with a thorough evaluation, they'll have all the information they need to make a buying choice. Readers will be persuaded to click on the link only if the review outperforms the quality of the merchant's sales page.

That is why comprehensive evaluations must be well researched and thorough to guarantee that you do not overlook any crucial things that the reader may be interested in. It's also a good idea to create YouTube affiliate marketing videos based on these in-depth product evaluations to expand the reach of your affiliate links.

Comparisons of Products

Product comparisons are another popular style for affiliate marketing product evaluations. They merely offer a product image, major features, and most likely, a star rating. The features and ratings are compared to those of other products in the same category to demonstrate how the product outperforms its competition.

These evaluations are often prepared in a tabular format, but we will not go into this further for the time being. Before you begin, you may want to look at some excellent product review examples. This will show you how successful affiliate sites organize their material.

Gather a few product review examples and expand on them to develop your own look.

How can you craft an unbiased product review for your affiliate marketing blog?

We cannot emphasize the term "honest" enough. To boost conversions with your affiliate marketing content, you need your audience's trust the most. Your audience will see through your product review if it sounds like another sales pitch.

An honest product review should make it seem as if you know what you're talking about. It should demonstrate your authority in the area as well as your product understanding. To guarantee that the affiliate products and companies you promote are of excellent quality, you should only join affiliate networks that prioritize quality above everything else.

Here are some pointers on how to write an honest affiliate product review.

Let's start with the facts.

The first and most essential thing to remember when writing a review for any product is to base your evaluation on facts. Begin with the information that the reader should be aware of. If you are writing an affiliate product review for a face cream, for example, you may begin by stating the components listed on the container.

If you are evaluating an electrical device, you must provide the product details. Rather than beginning with extraneous assertions that contribute nothing to the review, consider a brief introductory phrase followed by the facts.

Tell them why you bought it.

If you have utilized the product, you should inform your audience what led you to give it a try. This is possible even if you have never used the product. You should mention what the product promises to accomplish at this stage.

People are frequently enticed to purchase a product because of the pain points or consumer issues that it promises to remedy. You may list all of the benefits that the product promises to provide and explore them in depth in the following sections. You may also talk about how you found out about the product, whether it was via social media, an advertisement, or anything else.

It is also critical to be direct and honest here. If you have second thoughts about purchasing the goods, explain why to your viewers. Alternatively, if you believe it is lacking a common feature that you would want to see in a product like this, speak out about it.

Your audience must see you as one of them. The more relatable the review, the better your chances of connecting.

Please share your thoughts on the product.

After you've gathered all of the details, it's time to share your thoughts about the affiliate product. This is the most crucial part of every affiliate product review. You must provide your honest evaluation after utilizing the product in this section.

You are not required to discuss all of the aspects of a product/service here. Discuss the ones that your target audience would be most interested in. In addition to your textual review, it is critical to include product photos and videos in affiliate marketing content whenever possible.

After seeing a product picture or video, 62% of customers are more inclined to purchase a product. This is mostly because buyers want to see how a product appears in reality and whether it fits the description in the review. The photographs and videos of the goods posted by users provide the public a better impression of its quality, size, color, and material.

In addition to writing an honest review, it is critical that your audience be persuaded to click on your affiliate link. They will only do so if they believe the product is worth further investigation. So, while attempting to promote a product, even if subtly, you must present the product in a somewhat better light than its rivals.

It is critical that you discuss other products in the category and compare a few aspects of your product to these market competitors. It is not required for the product to excel in all of them. Discuss all of the benefits and downsides, but strive to emphasize a few extra advantages of the affiliate product over its competition.

It is critical that your audience be persuaded to click on your affiliate link

How do you submit product reviews for products you haven't tried or seen?

Before writing a product review for your affiliate blog, it is usually a good idea to purchase the product and use it for a time. However, we appreciate that certain things may be out of your price range or that you may not desire the product at all. However, this does not prevent anybody from posting a positive product review.

If you are unable to purchase the products, you must write a thorough and well-informed evaluation.

Conduct your research

The initial step will be to do extensive research. Look around the internet, visit other affiliate marketing sites in your field, or look for similar YouTube videos that contain detailed descriptions of the product.

Learn all you can about the product. A review cannot be a broad, superficial viewpoint. You must know more than the typical buyer based on what they see online.

Look for consumer feedback on e-commerce websites.

Look for the products elsewhere outside the merchant's website and check what customers have said in the reviews on these sites. Unlike other affiliate sites, user reviews on sites like Amazon will provide you with impartial opinions.

Pay attention to the websites of merchants and manufacturers.

Examine all of the facts on the merchant's sales page as well as the manufacturer's website. Typically, the product/service website will offer more than enough material to frame into an authentic-looking review. Look around to see if you can locate any more important information.

Even if you are not utilizing the product and are writing a product review for affiliate marketing, the goal should be to offer value to your consumers with whatever information you can supply.

What is the best way to write Amazon product reviews?

Amazon's affiliate marketing program is by far one of the most successful. So writing affiliate product reviews for Amazon items is not something you should think about, but rather something you should do. It is also vital to keep in mind that competition in Amazon product reviews will be fierce. As a result, your product reviews must be excellent.

Look for items that are related to your expertise.

Affiliate marketers must choose a niche and stick to it, regardless of how profitable other affiliate products seem to be. It is also critical that the Amazon products you pick to evaluate are relevant to your expertise. Not only will you be able to write better Amazon product reviews in your field of knowledge, but your readers will see you as an authority in the industry.

Look at Amazon to see what questions others have regarding the product.

The "Customer questions and answers" area on Amazon is a really handy tool. Through this function, people ask all types of questions about a product on every product page. Examine what people are asking.

This can aid your research while writing Amazon product reviews and offer you an idea of what shoppers want to know. Choose some key topics to mention in your Amazon product review from this list.

Learn what Amazon does not disclose about the product.

Your Amazon product review will only be useful if it contributes to the customer's decision-making process. They may have already heard what Amazon has to say about the products. You must inform them of what Amazon does not provide.

If you have used the product before, this will be no issue since you have firsthand knowledge. If you haven't used it before, do some further study. To learn more about the product, visit the manufacturer's website or other sites that have evaluated it.

What makes a decent product review template?

The product review's structure

The format of your product review determines whether people read it all the way through or quit it halfway through. An excellent product review template should look like this:

An eye-catching headline. However, avoid using clickbait. Be truthful from the outset. A brief overview. A few sentences should be sufficient. Only write what is useful and relevant. A link to the product on the merchant's website.

This is an excellent spot to include your affiliate link. It is usually preferable to utilize the anchor text as a CTA, such as "Buy it on merchantsite.com."

Features and specs are listed below. A bulleted list is the best approach to list all of the product's characteristics.

Product assessment. This is where you express your thoughts about the product. You may highlight some of the product's important features and describe how you believe it fared in these areas. This may be a couple paragraphs lengthy, with a subtitle for each important feature discussed.

There are benefits and drawbacks. This is your assessment of where the product excelled and where it fell short. Ensure to incorporate some drawbacks, striking a balanced tone without overlay.

Nothing is ever really perfect. When compared to other products in the same category. A reader may see your evaluation as prejudiced if you do not include any of the competitors.

Your ultimate decision. After all of this comparison, a reader may be curious about your ultimate thoughts on the product. This is your review's summary/conclusion. Tell the readers why you think this product is great.

Affiliate link placement

Another critical consideration when developing your product review template is where and how to include your affiliate links. Your review should include just enough affiliate links, but not too many. Stuffing affiliate links into your affiliate marketing article defeats the objective of creating an honest review.

That is one affiliate marketing content error you should never do. You may insert affiliate links in strategic places, such as soon after the introduction, as previously indicated. This may go one of two ways: the reader can click on the link if they don't want to read the whole review, or they can bypass the link and continue reading the review. In either scenario, you're in a win-win situation.

You may also include affiliate links in your post. You may include some clickable product photos that link to the product page. Alternatively, you could link the product titles in the article to the merchant site many times throughout the review.

A creative Call-to-Action (CTA) button is another effective approach to bring attention to the affiliate link. This might be near the conclusion of the review or wherever the reader will see it all the time.

How do you create an effective product review for SEO?

Your product reviews for affiliate marketing sites, like any other material, must be search engine optimized. To locate the most relevant terms in your area, you must do extensive keyword research. It is critical to have a keyword strategy and to use keywords naturally throughout your material. Here are a few pointers:

Create a list of core and secondary keywords and phrases. If feasible, use the primary keyword inside the first 150 characters, or at least in the first paragraph. Make sure the keywords are evenly distributed throughout the content. In the conclusion, use the primary keyword once or twice.

Short sentences and paragraphs should be used. Each paragraph should be no more than two to three sentences long. Use photos to break up the text and give enough white space to make your content more readable.

Make your product review easier to read by using additional bullet points, subheadings, numbered lists, and so on. When discussing the product's advantages and disadvantages, bullet points work best.

Finally, it is a good idea to have a FAQ section. Find some frequently asked questions about the product from clients and answer them succinctly below. When responding to FAQs, keep it brief.

Using an AI content generator to create affiliate marketing content may be a major benefit. These AI systems often include SEO capabilities that allow you to improve your content for search while also saving you time and effort.

The best methods for writing product reviews

a. Include a summary at the start.

The majority of reviewers do this in the form of a summary box or a TLDR (too long; do not read) section. In the summary, you should only summarize your thoughts on the product and perhaps provide a rating. This is for almost-decided customers who are searching for a fast second opinion.

They have all the information they want and are simply interested in knowing whether or not you suggest the product and why. Remember to include a CTA with your affiliate link at the conclusion of the summary so the reader does not have to scroll to locate the connection to the product page.

b. Feel sympathy for the audience.

Empathize with your audience to connect with them without coming off as a salesman for the products. Demonstrate that you comprehend the problem for which they are looking for a solution. Tell them you had the same situation, ideally with a brief explanation.

Your affiliate product review's wording and tone must be pleasant. Don't be too critical of any of the competitor items you mention. Try to be as objective as possible.

c. Inform those who should not purchase the goods.

Though the goal of a product review for affiliate marketing is to persuade the reader to purchase the product, it is also beneficial to suggest who should not consider purchasing it. Every product has a target consumer base, therefore identify who would benefit the most from the product. If you are evaluating a pair of pricey hiking shoes, you should inform your audience that they should only purchase them if they are frequent hikers.

People who do not participate in adventure sports or trekking will not be able to make the maximum use of these shoes, making them a waste of money. Instead, direct them to some of your other affiliate offerings. This way, you're establishing trust with an honest review, targeting the proper demographic, and directing them to your other affiliate product evaluations.

d.   Maintain consistency in your grading standards.

Ensure that you are consistent when assessing products based on their features or adding ratings to your reviews. If you use star ratings, use them consistently in all of your product reviews. Use the scale in all of them if you prefer to rate on a scale of 1 to 10.

Also, if you include grades for important features in your product evaluations, make sure you choose the same key features for products in the same category. This makes the ratings/grades simpler for readers to understand and compare.

Creating Engaging Blog Posts and Articles

Engaging blog content are essential for affiliate marketing success. It requires study, originality, and an awareness of what makes information interesting to write about anything and expect people to be engaged. Creating compelling blog entries that attract your target audience's attention takes time and effort. There's a lot more to developing powerful blogs than meets the eye, from researching subjects relevant to your niche market to adding graphic aspects for appeal.

Five technological suggestions for transforming your normal blog entries into a money-making machine.

a.   Always include a disclaimer on your blog.

There is one thing you must do before you begin marketing affiliate links. Remember to inform your followers that you get a percentage on every transaction made via your affiliate link. Declaring that you are compensated for advertising products or services via affiliate links may seem to be a bother, but it is the appropriate thing to do.

Gaining the trust of your audience is crucial for boosting sales in affiliate marketing. Your audience will not believe you if you conceal the fact that you are not advocating things in "good faith" but are being compensated for it. Furthermore, if you do not disclose your readers that you utilize sponsored links, you may face repercussions from affiliate program owners or regulatory authorities.

Declaring that you are compensated for advertising items or services via affiliate links is an appropriate thing to do

Being open and honest with your readers about receiving compensation to endorse a product creates trust and protects you from legal problems. Many followers prefer knowing that you are compensated from the start for evaluating products or services. It may even encourage them to click on your affiliate links.

The revelation does not have to be lengthy or complicated. It is sufficient to state that you are associated with a company and that you will be compensated if your viewers buy anything via the links in your postings. The disclaimer is also a great spot to clarify what an affiliate program is and how or why you choose the products or services you promote on your site.

In terms of where you should place the disclosure, the recommended practice is to put it at the top of your page. Make it simple for people to notice it before they come across any affiliate links.

b.   Take care not to seem too "salesy"

Of course, you want your viewers to click on your affiliate links and buy the things you're promoting. However, if you urge your readers to purchase the product by portraying it in superlatives and failing to discuss its drawbacks, you may come out as pushy. Nowadays, it is unusual to see a buyer purchase a product immediately after reading an advertising or suggestion.

The great majority of individuals do internet research and comparison shopping. If your audience spot errors in other reviews but none in yours, the odds of them clicking on your link and making a purchase are nil. And, certainly, pointing out problems in a product or service you're pushing increases the likelihood that your readers will not click on the link you're promoting.

Even if they are unable to purchase a product at this time, your next advice may be something they need. To do this, your readers must regard you as an impartial source of information rather than someone who exaggerates the advantages of a product in order to make a fast sale.

c.   Emphasize the advantages of the products you advocate.

Most of us do not consider the number of features while reading reviews or comparing goods. Instead, we want to know how the product will assist us in achieving a goal, solving an issue, or just making our lives simpler. For example, suppose you have a culinary blog and are evaluating a blender.

Writing about how many features the blender has won't teach your audience much. Isn't it much more persuasive to inform them they can make fresh, handmade smoothies in a matter of minutes without creating a mess in the kitchen? Even better if you can share your product-related experiences.

You may demonstrate how you utilized the blender to produce smoothies for a house party and the outcomes. You get extra points if you provide images of the creation process.

d.   Request promotional contents from the affiliate partner.

Sure, making a picture series or a video review of the offered products is a fantastic idea. However, creating them for each and every product you evaluate would take a significant amount of effort, and you would rapidly run out of ideas. Why not ask the owner of the affiliate program to share their promotional contents with you and use them in your blog post?

Assume they have a library of product visuals and banners, customer evaluations and case studies, or a series of video lectures. If that's the case, you might mix them with your images to produce fantastic product reviews or roundup blogs. It would be much more easy (for you and the affiliate products owner) if you could access a database including all accessible advertising products.

e.   Conduct keyword research

You must be visible in search engines if you want your blog entries to be discovered and read. And it is far from sufficient to post an article on your blog and maybe mention it on social media. If you want your article to rank, you must understand how to employ keywords effectively.

Aiming for short and common keywords may seem to be a smart idea since they are often searched for. However, since those keywords are so well-known, competition will be fierce. You don't want to get into a battle with the big names on those search results pages, believe me.

Looking for long-tail keywords relating to the product you're marketing is a far better idea. Typically, the number of searches for these particular terms is smaller. Nonetheless, you'll be able to attract buyers who are specifically seeking for the product you're promoting while facing much less competition. Add your primary keyword to Google and look at the recommendations at the bottom of the page to locate long-tail keywords.

Various keyword analytics tools are another great source of suggestions for more specialized search phrases. These answers may also inform you how much competition there is for a certain keyword.

Chapter 6: Mastering the Art of Promotion

"A man who stops advertising to save money is like a man who stops a clock to save time." – Henry Ford

Utilizing Email Marketing

Email marketing has been around for quite some time, but it is far from obsolete. In reality, it is still one of the most successful methods of reaching and engaging your target audience. In terms of affiliate marketing, email may be a game changer.

Steps to Affiliate Email Marketing

You must keep this friendly, conversational approach in mind when developing an affiliate marketing plan. Aside from that, you'll end up damaging your current customers' relationships and seeing your hard-earned email list dwindle due to unsubscribes.

a. **Sign up for an email service provider.**

To begin affiliate email marketing, you may sign up with an email service provider. While sending emails, it is essential to follow all applicable laws and regulations. You must first get permission from your subscribers before sending emails.

The term "implied consent" refers to the fact that you are already acquainted with the subscriber. A permission request requires express consent, demonstrating that you are unfamiliar with them and must have their explicit consent before contacting. Obtaining "explicit consent" is required when attempting to construct an affiliate marketing mailing list.

Don't forget about branding once you've chosen a service provider and email templates. Make your email template more visually appealing by using a logo and other branding features. If you don't already have a logo, consider making one using an online logo maker.

b. Send emails containing affiliate links

To begin, ensure that your email provider permits you to add affiliate links in your emails or that you may put the links in your signature using an email signature generator.

c. Communicate via Personalized Emails

Personalization is essential in affiliate emails in order to increase click rates. To be successful in affiliate marketing, you must cultivate connections with your target audience. Personalized emails will come out as more friendly than salesy.

Personalization is essential in affiliate emails in order to increase open rates

d. Monitor the affiliate emails

It worked well, and the commissions poured in. But wait, there's more. You must actively participate in order to continue receiving commissions. You must engage in some engagement in order to do this. To fine-tune your message, tag and monitor your subscribers as needed. Tracking and increasing open and click-through rates is made easier with audience segmentation.

e. Make the most of your vacation time.

The big holidays are anticipated by the public. So now is an excellent time to be innovative with your marketing. Increased disapproval rates will arise from overloading the subscribers. Make a Christmas advertisement as well. Be wary of your never-ending email list. Delete all holiday campaigns after the holiday season.

f. Start with the most crucial item.

Yes, email list affiliate marketing may be profitable, but value always comes first. Your target audience is looking for more than simply promotional contents. You may use videos, photos, audio, and podcasts to nurture your leads. It takes time and effort to build trust and closeness. If you give value, your subscribers will reward you with high affiliate commissions.

g. Make the most of their involvement.

Increasing your conversion rate requires re-engaging your leads. Send follow-up emails to those who have shown no interest. Your emails may not have been delivered. Alternatively, if you want to capitalize on a particularly profitable affiliate opportunity, such as a contest or higher commissions, try investing in a webinar platform and co-hosting a webinar with someone from the company. If you have a big enough audience, they will enjoy the additional exposure, and you will deliver genuine value.

h. Utilize social evidence and data.

Include success stories from customers who used the affiliate product you're marketing in your emails to give social proof to your database.

i. Keep in touch with your email subscribers.

Permission-based email marketers are the good guys. Every email subscriber who donates to your cause is handled with confidentiality and trust. Because of increased open rates and lower spam, they have more opportunity to build their business via email marketing.

j. Clearly indicate

When asking someone to join your list, be precise about the content you want to offer. Subscribers to your email list expect unique deals, promotions, and access to exclusive material.

k. Be mindful of your audience's privacy.

Trust is a key factor in determining whether or not someone will join your company. Post your privacy statement with caution. Even if the subscribers do not click on the link, your company and email will gain trust.

l. Do not overload your audience.

Don't pass up the chance to interact with your clients and prospects. Make sure your message is acceptable for your audience.

What to stay away from

Remember the most critical rule for using affiliate links even before you start your campaign. Many people argue that "the money is in the list," but the fact is that the money is in the relationship created with the list. Instead of continuously striving to sell or flood your email with affiliate links, the most important component of convincing readers to purchase anything is to first earn their trust, understand their demands, and present them with something of value.

This will keep your customers from getting annoyed with you. Furthermore, if you get too many link adverts, your email provider may terminate your account.

How should you proceed?

Include affiliate links among other crucial email information in your emails. You might even include them into an ongoing email campaign. Diversify your affiliate link placement, but keep in mind that everything is dependent on your viewership.

Eensure that affiliate links gives value and a solution for your viewers. A successful affiliate email marketing campaign will help to build trust and engagement, which is essential for growing sales since people are already acquainted with your fantastic content. This also means that more of your emails will be sent to the inbox rather than the Spam folder, resulting in increased income and good outcomes.

To make the process easier, you may also employ email marketing tools. These tools will enable you to produce customized content, collect feedback, conduct surveys, and send timely communications to customers while targeting the appropriate people at the right time.

Affiliate email marketing best practices

Let's look at the best practices you should always follow as an affiliate after we've examined how to correctly design an affiliate email marketing campaign that will increase your commissions.

a.   Sort through your email list.

Segmenting your list entails categorizing it based on your preferences and activities. Depending on the product you are selling and other considerations, you may only need to focus on a subset of your email list. Segmenting your list will not only increase your opt-ins, open rates, and conversion rates, but it will also let you to focus on each audience and give the right content to the right buyer at the right time.

b.   Utilize triggers.

Trigger emails are delivered to your audience in response to their actions. The majority of trigger emails, on the other hand, are segment-based or event-based. When your subscribers meet certain criteria, segment-based is utilized, while event-based is used when they opt-in or make a purchase.

Trigger emails are designed to provide support and nurturing to your customers so that they may completely benefit from the product. They are also used to transmit important information, contact information, and to promote good behavior.

c. Customize your emails

Individualized subject lines are 26% more likely to get opened in emails. This is especially important in affiliate email marketing, which is all about building trust between you and your customer base. When you send personalized emails, your list will regard you as a partner rather than a salesperson.

d. Improve email content

The efficacy of your affiliate email marketing plan is dependent by how effectively you exhibit professionalism to your target audience. Use your emails to promote yourself as a subject matter expert. People will take your ideas more seriously if they believe you are well-versed about the product.

Make your emails interesting by telling a story and painting a picture that will compel readers to purchase what you're offering.

Make your emails interesting by telling a story and painting a picture that will compel readers to purchase what you're offering

e. Increase the automation of your mailings.

Include automation in your affiliate email marketing plan. There is wonderful software available that can be used to send bulk emails, schedule mail-outs, and evaluate email engagement, such as Snov.io.

f. A/B split testin

A/B testing enables you to create two different emails and determine which one gets the most responses from your target audience. Affiliate email marketing is substantially more effective when programs are monitored and adjusted based on the best results.

Harnessing the Power of Social Media

Affiliate marketing has developed as a successful approach for boosting sales and creating money in the ever-changing digital world. The importance of social media, a strong channel for affiliate marketers aiming to grow their reach, interact with audiences, and increase their earning potential, is central to this transformation.

Social Media's Role in Affiliate Marketing

Social media has changed the landscape of affiliate marketing by providing a platform for marketers to engage with a large audience. Social media, unlike conventional marketing methods, provides for direct connection with prospective customers, allowing marketers to create trust and foster relationships that may lead to improved conversions.

Selecting the Best Platforms

When it comes to affiliate marketing, not all social media sites are made equal. Platforms with high interaction rates and visual appeal, such as Instagram, Pinterest, and Facebook, frequently provide greater results for affiliate marketers. The platform you choose should correspond to where your target audience spends the majority of their time and engages the most.

Creating an Effective Affiliate Marketing Social Media Strategy

Creating a Vibrant Social Presence

Understanding your audience's requirements and interests is the first step in establishing a strong social media presence. This entails crafting captivating content that connects with your audience while covertly inserting affiliate links. Building a significant presence requires consistency in posting, interaction, and honesty.

Using Content to Drive Affiliate Marketing

In the world of social media, content reigns supreme. This involves creating high-quality, useful, and interesting content that includes affiliate products or services organically. Affiliate links may be effectively integrated into how-to tutorials, product reviews, and lifestyle blogs pertaining to your subject.

Individual Social Media Platform Mastery

Instagram as an Affiliate Marketing Platform

Instagram's visual nature makes it an ideal platform for product promotion. Make use of high-quality images, interesting tales, and captivating descriptions. Influencer marketing and Instagram Shopping may also be used to boost conversion rates.

Facebook Affiliate Marketing Strategies

From building specialized pages and groups to running targeted advertisements, Facebook has several options to promote affiliate products. Regular postings, live videos, and interactive material that engages your audience may increase traffic to your affiliate links.

Engaging Your Audience to Improve Conversion

Building Trust with Your Audience Trust is an important aspect of affiliate marketing. Building a devoted following may be aided by being clear about your affiliate affiliations, offering honest evaluations, and responding to comments and messages.

Making Interactive and Interesting Content

Polls, quizzes, and Q&A sessions are examples of interactive content that may boost engagement. This involvement may lead to increased exposure for your content as well as improved click-through rates for your affiliate links.

Tracking and Measuring Success Analyzing and Optimizing Your Social Media Performance

The analytics tools supplied by social media sites might assist you in monitoring the success of your affiliate marketing activities. Metrics like engagement, click-through, and conversion rates are critical for determining the efficacy of your campaigns.

Adjusting Your Strategy

You may improve your performance by refining your strategy based on the data obtained. This might involve changing the sort of information you share, the frequency with which you post, or even the products you promote.

Adapting to Platform and Algorithm Changes

Keeping Up with Social Media Trends

Social media is ever-changing, with algorithms and user interfaces being updated on a regular basis. It is critical for affiliate marketers to remain up to date on these developments. Adapting your techniques to coincide with these adjustments might help your articles retain or even boost their exposure and engagement.

Taking Advantage of New Features and Technologies

Social media networks often roll out new services, such as Instagram Reels or Facebook Marketplace, that may be valuable tools for affiliate marketers. Embracing these new features early on may offer you a competitive advantage and enable you to interact with your audience in new and exciting ways.

Social Media and Affiliate Marketing Emerging Trends and Prospects

Using AI and Machine Learning

Artificial Intelligence (AI) and Machine Learning (ML) are changing the way marketers use social media. You may use these technologies to analyze massive data sets in order to better understand customer behavior, forecast trends, and customize content. AI solutions may also aid in the automation of tedious operations, enabling affiliate marketers to concentrate on strategy and content production.

Collaborations Between Influencers and Micro-Influencers

The emergence of influencers and micro-influencers is a goldmine for affiliate marketers. Collaborating with these social media influencers might help your campaigns get traction and credibility. Micro-influencers in particular have a highly engaged following, which makes them great partners for specialized companies.

Creating Effective Video Content for Affiliate Marketing

Video Content's Importance in Social Media

Because of its interesting and readily consumable format, video content has exploded in popularity on social media. TikTok, Instagram Reels, and YouTube Shorts are excellent platforms for generating short, captivating videos that efficiently market affiliate products.

The emergence of influencers and micro-influencers is a goldmine for affiliate marketers.

How to Make Engaging Video Content

Focus on narrative and authenticity to get the most out of video content. Videos don't have to be perfect; content that seems more authentic and relevant frequently performs better. To create a community around your content, demonstrate products, offer personal stories, and communicate with your viewers in the comments.

Analyzing and Improving Analytics for Social Media Performance and Understanding

Track the success of your posts and adverts using the analytics tools given by social media sites. Metrics like engagement rates, click-through rates, and conversion rates are critical for understanding your audience and improving future campaigns.

A/B Testing for Better Results

A/B testing allows you to experiment with alternative kinds of content, publishing schedules, and calls to action. This strategy enables you to examine several methods and determine which ones are most effective in engaging your audience and boosting affiliate sales.

Chatbots and Messaging Apps Integration

Using Chatbots to Improve Customer Experience

To increase customer connection, chatbots may be incorporated into social media sites. They respond quickly to inquiries, assist customers in making buying choices, and can even handle transactions, improving the entire user experience and boosting your affiliate marketing efforts.

Personalized Marketing via Messaging Apps

Messaging applications allow you to engage with your audience in a more intimate manner. You may utilize these platforms to create closer connections with your followers by communicating directly with them, delivering updates, and providing special offers relevant to your affiliate products.

Navigating Social Media Algorithm Changes for Affiliate Marketers

Keeping Up with Algorithm Updates

Social media companies' algorithms are routinely updated, affecting how information is presented and rated. Understanding these shifts is critical for affiliate marketers. Regular research and being up to speed on new developments will help you alter your plan properly. This might imply altering your posting frequency, content structure, or interaction strategies.

Creating Content That Is Algorithm-Friendly

Create content that corresponds with the platform's algorithm preferences to increase reach and engagement. This often contains material with a high level of engagement, such as videos, interactive postings (polls, questions), and content that stimulates significant conversations. Remember that engaging material is more likely to be preferred by algorithms.

The Storytelling Function in Social Media Affiliate Marketing

Using Stories to Engage Audiences

In social media marketing, storytelling is a valuable tool. It aids in the creation of a story for your affiliate items, making them more relevant and enticing. To develop a stronger connection with your audience, provide customer testimonials, behind-the-scenes glimpses, or personal experiences about the product.

Utilizing Instagram and Facebook Stories

Instagram Stories and Facebook Stories are excellent platforms for casual, entertaining storytelling. These elements may be used for time-limited deals, sneak peeks, or interactive content like as quizzes and polls, which can be quite useful in generating affiliate product interest.

Choosing Between Promotional and Non-Promotional Content

The Value of Content Variety

A successful social media affiliate marketing plan balances promotional and non-promotional content. Excessive marketing may turn off your audience, while a diversity of content kinds will keep them engaged and interested. Along with advertising material, include instructive, amusing, and informational pieces.

Engagement and User-Generated Content

To increase engagement and trust, encourage and distribute user-generated content (UGC). This might include customer reviews, testimonials, or images of them utilizing your affiliate products. Engaging your audience via comments, polls, and direct messaging may also help to build a devoted community and boost your marketing efforts.

Future-Proof Your Affiliate Marketing Strategy

a.   Keeping Up with New Platforms

The social media landscape is constantly evolving, with new platforms appearing on a regular basis. Keep an eye on new platforms and evaluate their suitability for your affiliate marketing plan. You may get a competitive edge by adopting technology early.

To increase engagement and trust, encourage and distribute user-generated content (UGC).

b.   Continuous Improvement and Adaptation

Commit to constant learning and adaptability to future-proof your affiliate marketing initiatives. Attend webinars, keep up with industry experts, and test out new approaches and technologies. The terrain will continue to change, and adaptability is essential for long-term success.

Exploring Paid Advertising Options

a.   Understanding the Basics of Paid Advertising Using Paid Social Media Advertising Effectively

Paid social media advertising may extend your reach and target particular audiences more effectively than organic techniques alone. Facebook and Instagram, for example, provide advanced targeting options based on demographics, hobbies, and activity, making your affiliate marketing efforts more targeted and successful.

b.   Creating Interesting Ad Content

The success of sponsored advertisements is heavily dependent on the content. Ads should be visually beautiful, have captivating language, and, most importantly, be relevant to the target audience's interests and requirements. Different ad formats and creatives may be tested to see what performs best for your affiliate products.

Harnessing the power of paid advertising in the fast-paced world of affiliate marketing may catapult your efforts to new heights. Paid advertisements provide tailored exposure, enabling you to reach particular audiences interested in the things you're marketing.

a.   **Select the proper Advertising Platform**: Choosing the proper advertising platform is the first step in running paid advertisements for affiliate marketing. Google Ads, Facebook Ads, Instagram Ads, Twitter Ads, and more options are available. To make an educated selection, consider your target demographic, the nature of the items you're marketing, and the platform's ad structure.

b.   **Understand Your Target demographic**: Paid advertising success is dependent on a thorough grasp of your target demographic. Define their demographics, hobbies, and internet habits. This data will determine the settings of your ad targeting, ensuring that your adverts reach the most appropriate and responsive audience.

c. **Choose Relevant Keywords**: When utilizing platforms such as Google Ads, keywords play an important role in ad exposure. Perform keyword research to find phrases related to the affiliate items you're marketing. Include a combination of short-tail and long-tail keywords to reach a large yet targeted audience.

d. **Write Captivating Ad text**: Your ad text is your first point of contact with prospective customers. Create interesting, short, and appealing ad text that promotes the affiliate goods' advantages. Highlight your unique selling features and utilize language that is appealing to your target audience.

e. **Make Use of High-Quality Visuals**: Visuals are effective instruments in paid advertising. Use high-quality graphics that present the affiliate items in the greatest light, whether they be images or videos. Make sure your images are consistent with the overall narrative and branding of your campaign.

f. **Use Conversion monitoring**: Conversion monitoring is critical for determining the performance of your paid advertising efforts. Set up tracking pixels or tags to track important behaviors like clicks, sign-ups, and sales. This information is crucial for improving campaigns and increasing return on investment (ROI).

g. **Optimize Landing Pages**: The effectiveness of an ad is only as good as the landing page it leads to. Ensure that your landing pages are conversion-optimized. The page should be consistent with the theme of the advertisement, give clear information, and feature a compelling call-to-action (CTA).

h. **Retargeting** is an effective tactic that includes presenting adverts to visitors who have previously engaged with your website or ads. Retargeting pixels may be used to re-engage customers by reminding them of the affiliate products they saw and prompting them to take the required action.

i. **Establish a Reasonable Budget**: Establish a reasonable budget for your paid advertising initiatives. Consider aspects such as cost per click (CPC), conversion rates, and campaign length. Begin with a small budget and gradually increase it as you collect data and optimize for greater performance.

j. **Experiment with Ad Formats**: Different ad formats appeal to different types of audiences. Experiment with several formats, such as picture advertisements, video ads, carousel ads, and narrative ads, to see what works best for your target demographic. Platforms often give data about the success of various ad types.

k. **Analyze and monitor performance metrics**: Monitor the performance of your sponsored ad campaigns on a regular basis. Metrics including click-through rate (CTR), conversion rate, cost per conversion, and return on ad spend (ROAS) should be monitored. Analyzing this data allows you to find effective techniques as well as opportunities for improvement.

l. **Stay Up to Date on Ad Policy Changes**: Ad platforms constantly adjust their rules. Keep up to date on any changes to ad rules to ensure your campaigns stay compliant. Noncompliance might lead to advertising being rejected or account suspension.

Which is preferable: sponsored or free traffic?

At first look, it may seem like free traffic is preferable since, well, it's free! Everyone appreciates something they don't have to pay for, but there must be a catch, right? The problem with optimizing your affiliate marketing content just for free visitors is that it takes a long time to see significant development. With so many other content providers releasing identical content on the same themes, it's no surprise that establishing a consistent stream of free visitors might take time. People who like free traffic frequently devote effort in learning the finest SEO tactics.

While we encourage optimizing your affiliate marketing material for free traffic via SEO, you may also profit from exploring paid marketing options.

The advantages of using sponsored traffic marketing methods

After putting in the effort to create exceptional affiliate marketing content, it only makes sense to optimize it for increased traffic and sales via paid marketing channels. Then you may use what you've learned to create further affiliate content.

Here are a few reasons why you should focus more on paid marketing.

a.   Increased growth

As previously said, generating free traffic via SEO takes time. Consider how much competition you have from other long-standing websites with higher domain authority than you. With so many variables involved in obtaining regular free traffic, investing in bought traffic solutions might assist you in avoiding this stage. Rather than waiting months or even years for any type of development, you can begin improving your affiliate marketing content now and get results nearly immediately. With the touch of a few clicks, you can get your affiliate marketing material in front of your target audience when you invest in PPC advertisements (pay-per-click advertising).

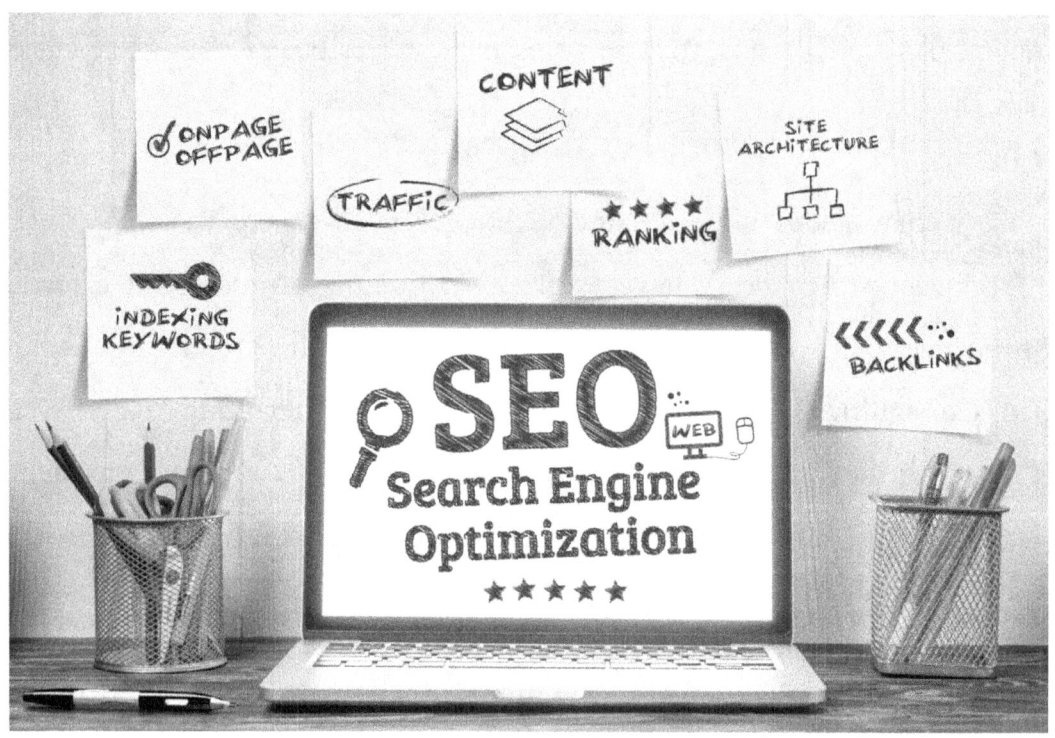

Generating free traffic via SEO takes time

There's no need to wait for your content to rank higher in Google or get traction on social media. You will notice progress instantly!

b.   Improved ad targeting

When you optimize your affiliate marketing content just for SEO, you risk attracting people that aren't from your target demographic. Assume you're creating an affiliate blog article for a calendar scheduling service you like. You publish the blog article, and over time, you see an increase in free traffic to your site via automatic social network postings and organic Google searches.

This seems to be a good thing until you learn that the folks who click on your blog article are merely doing research and do not really click your affiliate link to purchase a tool subscription.

Perhaps you've seen that the majority of individuals looking for a calendar scheduling tool are typical career professionals in medical care, but you'd want to target stay-at-home parents who need to categorize their to-do list and organize their schedule.

c.   **It's giving you more traffic, but it's not the correct type.**

You want highly targeted traffic that will not only deliver you a one-time affiliate transaction but will also convert that person into a regular reader or follower. This is something that sponsored marketing may acquire you in a very short period of time. Visitors are more likely to convert into purchases.

How long does it take to make affiliate content?

Because time is your most important resource, you don't want to waste it on ventures that don't pay off. Affiliate marketing may be incredibly profitable, but it generally takes some trial and error before you see a significant quantity of revenue come in. Instead of getting caught up in the grind of attempting to gain views on your affiliate marketing content, you can concentrate on what will best convert your target audience with paid marketing. Paid advertisement has already taken care of that!

Greater conversions equate to greater revenue.

This is especially beneficial for affiliate programs that provide you with monthly recurring earnings for the life of any account acquired via your affiliate link. That implies you might get a monthly payment from affiliate programs. That is certainly passive income!

You don't have to spend a lot of money.

One of the most popular misunderstandings about paid marketing is that it requires a huge financial commitment before you see any form of return. Many social media and search engine paid marketing platforms allow you to get started with sponsored advertising for as little as a few dollars. When you initially start out, you don't need to spend a lot of money on sponsored promotion.

Instead, start small and test your ad targeting, wording, and graphics to ensure they are optimal for your target demographic. You'll have a simpler time turning visitors into qualified leads as you demonstrate which adverts are worth investing paid marketing money in. When establishing a new paid marketing campaign, we usually suggest starting with split testing (which pits several variants of an ad against one other to discover which works better).

When planning your paid marketing approach, set aside a tiny portion of your money to experiment with. If you are a sole proprietor or manage a small firm, don't be concerned about investing hundreds or thousands of dollars in paid advertising. Even if you just invest $10 each week for a few months, you will learn a lot!

Affiliate marketing's best paid traffic sources

When considering purchased traffic for promoting your affiliate content, we must determine which platforms will provide the most return. We don't want to invest in a platform that doesn't cater to our target demographic or provide the best outcomes. While testing your sponsored advertising is a terrific approach to determine which platform is ideal for you, let's make sure we do our homework and make an educated selection.

Here are some of the most popular paid traffic sources for affiliate marketing, as well as reasons why they can be a good match for you.

AdWords by Google

Google Adwords is the company's paid advertising platform. When you type a search query into Google, you'll notice that one to three adverts appear at the top of the search results page before the organically ranked website pages. This helps you to optimize your paid adverts for individuals who are currently searching for comparable terms on Google.

Who it's for: Given that Google accounts for 77% of all internet searches, it's fair to assume that Google Adwords may be a good match for almost any business or content provider! Because so many people already use Google, you can meet them where they are.

Why use it: Before making a buying choice, most individuals use a search engine. This is because consumers believe Google will provide them with the most appropriate response to their query. It's an excellent location to test your affiliate marketing ad targeting.

Ads on Facebook

What it is: Given that Facebook is the most popular social media site, it's no wonder that they have the biggest social media advertising platform. With its unique, updated features, it provides some of the greatest audience targeting possibilities available.

Who it's for: Facebook is popular among people of all ages. You're bound to discover individuals in your target market on Facebook, which has 2.2 billion active members. Facebook Ads provides comprehensive targeting capabilities, allowing you to target your affiliate marketing content to a highly specific demographic.

Facebook have the biggest social media advertising platform

Why use it: Facebook Ads allow you to post a hidden Facebook Pixel on your website in order to attract the attention of individuals who have previously visited your website (this is known as retargeting). Someone who has heard of you previously is simpler to convert than someone who has never heard of you.

Facebook advertisements also allows you to target your advertisements based on which Facebook pages people like, which groups they belong to, and other Facebook-specific information.

Instagram advertisements

What it is: Instagram, which is owned by Facebook, has also grown into a social media behemoth, particularly in the past five years with the launch of Instagram Stories and Instagram Live. With so many features, Instagram is skillfully monetizing its developing platform with Instagram Ads.

Who it's for: Because Instagram is designed for visual folks, it has over 600 million active users on its site. Instagram has quickly become a Millennial favorite, with 59% of 18-29 year olds using it.

Why should you utilize it: Instagram Ads might be a wonderful area to start experimenting if your affiliate marketing material is mainly visual and you're aiming to target a younger population. You may develop Instagram Ads with varied aims in mind, such as increasing interaction or driving sponsored visitors.

Influencer Promotion

What it is: Influencer marketing is distinct in that it is not limited to a single search engine or social media advertising platform. An influencer, defined as someone who motivates a big number of people to take action, may promote affiliate products almost anyplace. Influencer marketing might be a good match for you if you are developing your own brand and want to make affiliate marketing one of your major sources of revenue.

Who it's for: Influencer marketing is usually for those who have a huge following on certain social media sites or via their website, but as a micro-influencer, you can also make amazing affiliate marketing material.

Why should you utilize it: As an influencer, you may experiment with various forms of paid marketing channels knowing that you already have a captive audience. People are more likely to click on your affiliate ad and purchase from you if they already know your identity and trust you. This type of impact is priceless!

How to Use Paid Traffic for Affiliate Marketing Successfully

After you've tried a few bought traffic sources, you can start thinking about how to leverage each platform to maximize your affiliate marketing profits. Here are some excellent practices to remember as you embark on your paid advertising adventure with affiliate marketing content development.

Target the Right Audience

Choose the appropriate audience.

You should devote as much effort as possible to locating the correct targeted audience for your ad as you do to writing and creating it. Too many individuals speed through ad targeting, although it is the single most important factor in determining the effectiveness of your campaign (together with visuals). You will not get big results if your ad does not reach the right individuals.

We suggest devoting enough time to the targeting step. It may take some trial and error to get it exactly right. Don't be hesitant to experiment with different targeting settings until you discover one that works for you. If you want to put more effort into identifying the most lucrative targeting, you may hire a professional traffic consultant later on.

However, you might begin by doing your own sponsored advertisements at first.

Keyword Analysis

Keyword research

Are you targeting the proper keywords? This is particularly true for search engine platforms such as Google AdWords. If you use the incorrect keywords, you risk reaching the wrong audience or failing to provide visitors with appropriate affiliate marketing content. Consider the phrases and keywords that are most often used in your niche while trying to locate the perfect keywords.

These are referred to as "niche keywords" since they are particular to your sector. Before deploying them, make sure they fit the search purpose behind your affiliate marketing content topics. You may also launch Google and begin trying various keywords in the auto-complete search field.

It will show you many alternatives so you can see what is most often searched for. Continue to test and adjust.

Test and Adjust

Adjust and test

We've previously discussed the importance of testing, tweaking, and experimenting with your paid marketing initiatives, but we couldn't close this piece without emphasizing it again. Don't stress about getting your paid ad text, design, and targeting quite right the first time. The finest advertisements are the product of ongoing development and optimization.

What paid traffic channel are you going to begin utilizing for affiliate marketing?

Now that you've learned about some of the best paid marketing channels, it's time to put them to use in your affiliate marketing. Choose one now and begin planning a campaign for your company.

Combining Email Marketing and Social Media Strategies

Using Social Media to Build an Email List

Your social media following might be a goldmine for growing an email list. You may promote sign-ups by providing incentives such as exclusive material, discounts, or early product access. An email list complements your social media efforts by allowing for more direct and tailored engagement with your audience.

Using Email Marketing to Increase Affiliate Sales

Email marketing may be used to nurture leads, give helpful information, and more directly promote affiliate products. Using user behavior and preferences to segment your email list might result in improved open rates and conversions for your affiliate marketing efforts.

Navigating Legal Issues and Ethical Practices

Understanding Affiliate Disclosure Laws

Transparency regarding affiliate links is not just ethical, but also required by law in many jurisdictions. Make sure you understand and follow the Federal Trade Commission (FTC) rules or comparable legislation in your country, which frequently demand explicit disclosure of affiliate links in social media postings.

Keeping Authenticity and Trust

While it is necessary to promote affiliate products, it is also critical to prioritize your audience's trust. This includes promoting items in which you actually believe and avoiding anything that is deceptive or unduly promotional. Maintaining this equilibrium is critical to long-term success in affiliate marketing.

Part C: Navigating the Affiliate Landscape
Chapter 7: Understanding Affiliate Networks

Navigate the affiliate network marketplace, learn popular ones, and maximize your revenues with wise program selection.

Chapter 8: Analyzing and Improving Performance

Dive into analytics tools, monitoring and assessing campaign results, and altering plans for continual optimization.

Chapter 9: Scaling Your Affiliate Marketing Business

Learn how to grow your company by outsourcing tasks, extending your product line, and diversifying revenue sources for long-term success.

Chapter 7: Understanding Affiliate Networks

"Your network is your net worth." – **Tim Sanders**

Overview of Popular Affiliate Networks

An affiliate network is a service that links businesses with affiliates. The network serves as a "middleman," allowing affiliates and companies providing affiliate marketing programs to easily locate one another. Affiliates may be recruited and contracted by brands to market their products and create a new sales channel. Affiliate networks are often used by brands when:

- More outbound sales assistance is required.

- Have a limited advertising budget.

- Want to reach a new audience

Publishers (affiliates) benefit from affiliate networks because they make it easier to identify programs and handle affiliate revenue distributions. They simplify the process of identifying and dealing with affiliates for brands. Creators may find and join hundreds of programs, enabling them to promote items and make affiliate sales on a larger scale than if they signed up for several programs individually.

How do affiliate networks function?

Affiliate networks link affiliate marketers with brands, assisting both parties in managing their affiliate activity. As an affiliate, you just join the network to have access to products on the market. Some networks have stringent standards for affiliates to join, and you may be denied membership if you do not meet them.

AvantLink, for example, verifies for site ownership and does a human inspection. Other affiliate marketing networks, such as **ShareASale**, are suitable for newcomers owing to features such as rapid signups and the ability to start generating sales within minutes.

Joining and Navigating Affiliate Programs

Affiliate networks may link you to hundreds, if not thousands, of companies. As a result, they are one of the simplest methods to monetize a site or generate passive income. Here are some more advantages of joining an affiliate network:

- There is no need to pursue money; the platform will do it for you.
- Choose products or services that are relevant to your target audience.
- Some affiliate networks provide incentives and awards, so the more you sell, the higher your commission rates may be.
- You will have access to analytics and reporting tools to monitor your success.

Affiliate networks have several drawbacks. Some, for example, provide very low commission rates or demand sites to have a certain level of traffic before applying. Overall, they may be an effective technique to monetise website visits.

Top Affiliate Networks to Think About

Enter "affiliate networks" into Google and you'll find hundreds of platforms to pick from, some legitimate and others suspicious. So, how do you choose the best one? Begin by assessing your target audience. What kinds of products and services are likely to pique your readers' interest?

For example, digital marketers are more likely to be interested in SEO tools than women's fashion, therefore I may choose an affiliate network that connects me to online tools and marketing analysis platforms.

When evaluating the best affiliate networks, keep the following factors in mind:

- How much will you make in commissions each sale? Networks may differ greatly.
- Choosing a product or service: Will the network introduce you to companies that your target audience will be interested in?
- Requirements for approval: Some networks demand that your site be well-established or have a specific level of traffic.
- Other charges: Some affiliate networks charge training or setup fees.
- Cookie duration: Cookie length relates to how long a program monitors and credits you for a potential customer. Durations might vary greatly across platforms. Amazon, for example, has a cookie lifespan of 24 hours, but Avangate has a cookie duration of 120 days.

Let's look at some of the best affiliate marketing networks now that you know what to search for - and what to avoid.

ShareASale (https://www.shareasale.com/info/)

This Chicago-based affiliate network has been in operation since the year 2000. As a ShareASale associate, you can connect with over 4,000 programs and earn money on a variety of products from Reebok to Cricut to Etsy. This is one of the biggest affiliate marketing companies, and their commission rates are quite competitive.

However, the interface may be difficult to use, so I recommend taking advantage of the training they provide.

Rate of commission: varies per merchant; averages between 5% and 20%.

Product Types: A wide variety of products are available, including accessories, apparel, art, computers, automobiles, and even online dating services.

Best for: Affiliate publishers that are new or established and want to market tangible products.

Awin (https://www.awin.com/gb)

Awin is a worldwide affiliate network platform with over 15,000 advertisers that helped earn over $150 million in sales in 2019. It's also worth mentioning that they control numerous other affiliate networks, like ShareASale, which have their own websites. As Awin is one of the largest affiliate networks, it's worth considering.

They offer access to a wide range of merchants, including StubHub, Hyatt, AliExpress, and UnderArmour. Though trustworthy, they do charge a $5 application fee. It is more of a deposit, as it gets credited to your account if you are approved.

Still, it can be a little off-putting. You also have to apply to each program separately, which can be a bit of a hassle.

- **Commission Rate:** Varies by merchant, but averages around 5%

- **Product Types**: Huge variety, including travel, fashion, technology, finance, insurance, and e-commerce

- **Best For**: Newbies or established affiliate marketers

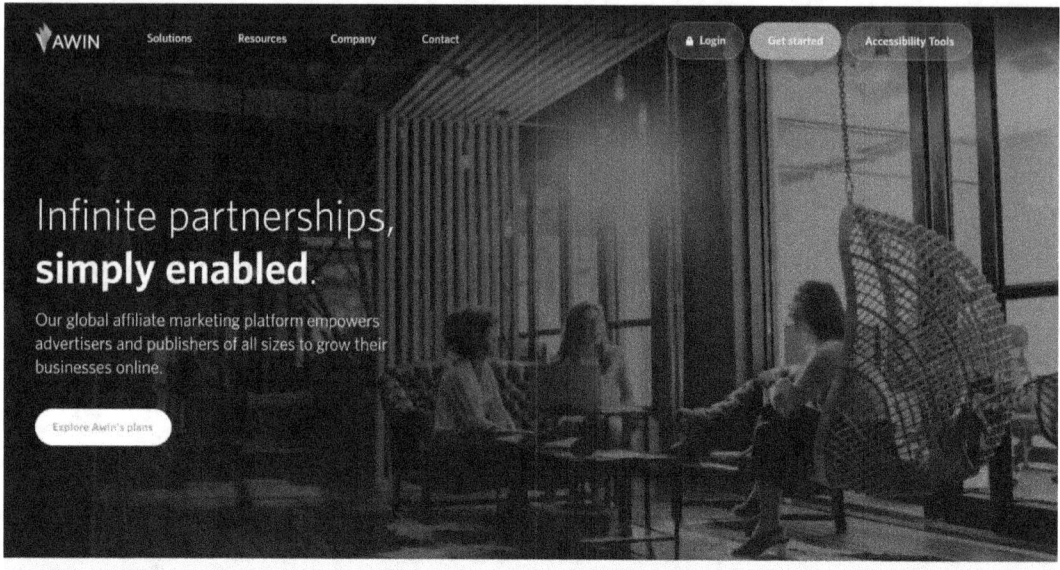

Awin is a worldwide affiliate network platform with over 15,000 advertisers that helped earn over $150 million in sales in 2019

Amazon Associates (https://affiliate-program.amazon.com/)

Amazon Associates is perhaps the most well-known affiliate network. Amazon, the world's biggest e-commerce shop, gives access to millions of items ranging from baby gear to home goods, beauty, and much more. The platform is simple to use, and getting started takes just a few minutes.

Furthermore, you may earn a commission on any product purchased by your audience in the following 24 hours, not just the ones you share. However, their terms and conditions may be rather severe, and their commission rates are often smaller than those of most other platforms.

Commission Rate: 5%; varies according on product type

Product Types: Almost every tangible commodity you can think of: gardening, school, reading, cuisine, home products, fashion, accessories, cosmetics, and so on.

Ideal For: All types of affiliate marketers

CJ Affiliate (https://www.cj.com/)

CJ Affiliate, formerly known as Commission Junction, is one of the world's biggest and oldest affiliate marketing networks. They link businesses with over 14 billion readers each year and help affiliate marketers earn over $1.8 billion. They're a huge issue in the affiliate marketing industry, and it's simple to understand why.

CJ Affiliate collaborates with hundreds of companies, including household names such as Lowe's, Barnes & Noble, Priceline, and Overstock. Overall, their approval procedure is rather quick, and there are no application costs. Earnings per click (EPC) is used to rate each product.

There are a couple drawbacks: you'll need clearance from each store before you can begin marketing, and you may be refused. In addition, if you do not make a transaction within six months, your account may be terminated.

Commission Rate: The commission rate varies depending on the merchant.

Product Categories: Include retail, software, travel, and finance.

Recommended for: Mid-level to seasoned affiliates

Rakuten Advertising (https://rakutenadvertising.com/)

Rakuten Advertising, founded as a Japanese e-commerce firm, is home to one of the biggest affiliate marketing networks. Affiliates may have access to hundreds of major companies, like Wells Fargo, Lilly Pulitzer, Virgin Holidays, and Ecco. However, they do not make it simple to join up. You must first join their affiliate network before signing up for and being accepted by any merchant program you want to join. You must also have an existing website.

The Commission Rate: Varies depending on the merchant.

Product Categories: Retail, D2C (Direct-to-Consumer), banking, travel, and other product types

Best For: Experienced affiliate marketers with consistent traffic.

Avangate Affiliate Network (https://www.avangatenetwork.com/)

Avangate Affiliate Network links publishers with digital products merchants such as software and digital security firms such as Malwarebytes. Blue Book Global has recognized them as the #1 WorldWide Affiliate Network for the previous six years. They offer one of the market's longest cookie lengths of 120 days and enable affiliates to develop discounts to assist boost purchases. The reporting options, however, are quite restricted.

Commission Rate: Starts at 25% and may rise to more than 50% for certain merchants.

Product Types: Digital products such as security and SaaS (Software as a Service).

For: Publishers in the technology, business, SaaS, or allied areas.

ClickBank (https://www.clickbank.com/)

ClickBank is a worldwide affiliate marketing network that gives you access to a diverse choice of products to promote, both physical and digital. Overall, ClickBank is simple to use and offers a diverse selection of products. Check out products before promoting them, however, since not all offered products are of great quality.

Their free training tools are also quite limited, despite the fact that they have a premium training platform called ClickBank University.

Commission Rate: Up to 90%, however most are somewhat lower.

Product Types: A wide range of products are available, including arts and entertainment, business, marketing, gaming, parenting, health and fitness, languages, and self-help.

Best For: Affiliate marketers at all levels that wish to promote largely tangible products.

FlexOffers

FlexOffers links publishers with over 12,000 ad programs and 500 premium advertisers. They, like many of the major affiliate networks, provide access to a vast array of products such as automobile, clothes, accessories, technology, education, health, and home & garden. Every publisher is also allocated a dedicated account manager, and the approval procedure is rapid.

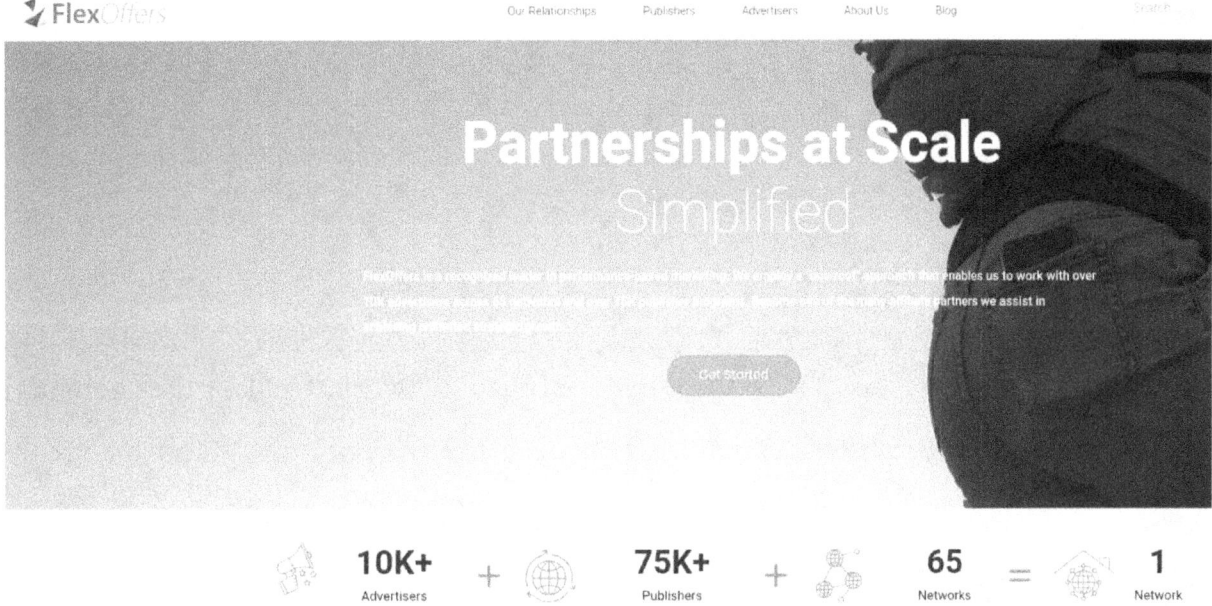

FlexOffers links publishers with over 12,000 ad programs and 500 premium advertisers.

Commission Rate: The commission rate varies depending on the merchant.

Product Types: Most are tangible, but others are digital.

Best for: Affiliates of all levels, from novice to experienced.

Sovrn//Commerce (https://www.sovrn.com/commerce/)

Sovrn//Commerce, formerly known as VigLink, is a top-tier publishing network that links publishers with hundreds of retailers. They accomplish this automatically by connecting you to the merchant with the greatest commission utilizing natural language processing. They also give precise performance analytics to assist you in increasing conversions.

The site also links publishers with possibilities for sponsored content.

Commision Rate: The commission rate varies depending on the merchant.

Product Types: Some digital, largely physical things such as skincare, household goods, sporting products, clothes, and accessories.

Ideal For: All affiliate marketers that have a blog.

JVZoo (https://www.jvzoo.com/)

With over 800,000 active affiliates, JVZoo is a major affiliate network. Unlike other networks that enable you to promote a broad variety of products, the majority of JVZoo merchants work in marketing, technology, and artificial intelligence. JVZoo offers automatic payouts and an easy-to-use dashboard to help you monitor your progress.

Commission Rate: The merchant's commission rate varies.

Product Types: Digital goods in the sectors of internet marketing, artificial intelligence, training, and finance.

Best For: IT, AI, and digital marketing affiliates.

SKIMLINKS (https://skimlinks.com/)

SKIMLINKS works with publishers to create affiliate links for merchants automatically. This means you can concentrate on creating outstanding content while SKIMLINKS handles the rest. They partner with over 60,000 publications, including well-known brands such as HuffPost, Conde Nast, and Yahoo! Simply join up, embed their Javascript on your website, and begin earning commissions.

While you may have less control over what you promote, it is a simple method to generate affiliate cash.

Commission Rate: The commission rate varies depending on the merchant.

Product Types: Mostly tangible things in fields such as apparel and technology, although certain digital products such as dating applications are also available.

Ideal for: Large affiliates, but also works well for those just getting started.

Maximizing Earnings Through Networks

Affiliate marketing is a tried-and-true technique to make money online, and the key to increasing your profits is to earn big commissions. You may dramatically increase your revenue potential by working with organizations that provide large commission rates. High commissions are essential in affiliate marketing because they incentivize affiliates to promote items and services.

You may dramatically increase your revenue potential by working with organizations that provide large commission rates

Affiliates are driven to put in more effort to grow sales and attract clients when they get larger commissions. This may result in higher brand exposure and revenue for businesses. If an affiliate earns a large commission for marketing a fitness product, they may devote more time and resources to developing interesting content and advertising campaigns.

As a consequence, the company's conversion rate will increase, resulting in more revenue. As a result, big commissions are an effective motivator and incentive for affiliates, eventually benefitting both parties engaged in the affiliate marketing process. In the field of affiliate marketing, high commissions for affiliates provide considerable benefits.

If an affiliate earns a large commission for marketing a fitness product, they may devote more time and resources to developing interesting content and advertising campaigns. As a consequence, the company's conversion rate will increase, resulting in more revenue. As a result, big commissions are an effective motivator and incentive for affiliates, eventually benefitting both parties engaged in the affiliate marketing process.

In the field of affiliate marketing, high commissions for affiliates provide considerable advantages. Affiliates are encouraged to market items or services that pay larger commissions because of the lucrative prospects they provide. For example, as affiliates earn larger commissions, they may spend more in their campaigns, improving their reach and conversion potential.

Choosing High Commission Affiliate Programs.

Looking for High Commission Programs in the Industry.

When starting out in the world of affiliate marketing big commissions, studying the business is a must. Understanding the market conditions and prospective programs accessible may have a significant influence on one's performance. Consider the case of a marketer specializing in health and wellness items.

They may uncover profitable programs in the shape of weight reduction pills, vitamin subscriptions, or fitness equipment by performing extensive study. This information enables them to target certain products with high commission rates and the potential for big revenue. Marketers may find lucrative prospects and customize their strategy by researching the sector.

Identifying High Commission Programs for Specific Niches

When it comes to selecting niche-specific high commission programs in affiliate marketing, significant study and analysis are required. Marketers may locate programs that give high commissions and fit with the interests of the target niche by researching into it and knowing its particular requirements and preferences. Because of the great demand for these products in the health and wellness sector, programs concentrating on supplements, workout equipment, or specific diets may pay larger commissions.

Furthermore, it is beneficial to investigate affiliate networks and directories that organize programs based on different categories, enabling marketers to simply locate high commission chances without having to sift through several platforms.

Taking Advantage of Product Quality and Brand Reputation

Using product quality and brand reputation to maximize high rewards via affiliate marketing is a vital technique. Customers are more inclined to believe recommendations and make a purchase when products of exceptional quality and a strong brand reputation are promoted. For example, a well-known sports shoe brand provides outstanding comfort, durability, and style, drawing devoted consumers prepared to pay a premium price.

Similarly, a well-known electronics business with a reputation for cutting-edge technology and excellent customer service may increase sales via affiliate marketing. You may easily increase your chances of earning larger commissions by linking yourself with products that stand out in terms of quality and reputation.

Strategies for Increasing Affiliate Marketing Income

Conversion Rate Optimization for High Commission Programs

Optimizing conversion rates for large commission programs is a critical component of affiliate marketing success. Marketers may increase their chances of turning leads into paying clients by using effective techniques. Implementing engaging call-to-actions and faster checkout procedures, for example, may drastically enhance conversion rates.

Incorporating compelling copywriting tactics, such as the scarcity principle or social proof, may also boost conversions. A well-optimized website with easy navigation and a visually attractive design is also important in motivating visitors to take action. Marketers may optimize conversions and produce larger commissions by concentrating on these practical strategies.

Creating a Specific Audience

Building a focused audience is critical for optimizing affiliate marketing revenue. You boost your chances of turning leads into sales by finding and targeting the correct audience. If you're offering a fitness product, for example, targeting folks who have recently shown an interest in fitness via their online activity might be beneficial.

Similarly, if you're offering a personal finance service, targeting those who have looked for financial planning advice might be beneficial. You may improve your affiliate marketing approach and eventually boost your earnings by targeting your marketing efforts to certain demographics, interests, and behaviors.

Continuous Performance Monitoring and Analysis

In the realm of high commission affiliate marketing, it is critical to constantly measure and analyze success. Marketers may acquire significant insights into the efficacy of their campaigns by regularly monitoring key indicators such as click-through rates, conversion rates, and average order values. This data-driven strategy enables them to make sound judgments and improve their plans for optimum profit.

Analyzing the success of multiple landing pages, for example, may indicate which ones are producing the most conversions, allowing marketers to deploy their resources appropriately. Furthermore, by monitoring performance over time, marketers may find trends and patterns that can be used to drive future campaign changes and improvements.

Chapter 8: Analyzing and Improving Performance

"Affiliate marketing isn't a get-rich overnight scheme. It will take some time before you'll see the results." —
David Sharpe

Introduction to Analytics Tools

All contemporary firms that are successful are founded on a strong foundation of data collection and analysis. This allows organizations to assess client preferences and behavior, as well as forecast future consumer behaviors. Affiliate marketers are no different; using data to simplify and enhance their plan will help them produce more traffic and conversions.

Unfortunately, just measuring the quantity of sales generated by your affiliate approach is insufficient. To successfully include data analysis into your plan, you must go deeper into the figures to get more specific insights into how your strategy is operating. A variety of tools are available to affiliate marketers to help them execute a data-driven strategy.

Let's have a look at several and talk about what they have to offer.

a. **Google Analytic**

For good reason, Google Analytics is frequently the first thing that springs to mind when people think about data analysis. Google's analytic system transformed how internet platforms see and utilize data, and it became a fundamental component in how tactics are conceived and evolved. Google debuted Universal Analytics, its flagship service, in 2012, providing users with never-before-seen insights into client behavior.

Google recently announced the release of their improved analytics system, Google Analytics 4 (GA4), which includes a number of new features and functionalities that improve on its predecessor. GA4 has an entirely new measurement approach based on events rather than page views. Interactions like browsing, clicking, searching, and interaction are recorded as events, providing a considerably more thorough picture of client activity.

The redesigned user interface allows users to monitor specific events and interactions, as well as specify custom settings and critical performance indicators. Furthermore, GA4 can monitor data across numerous platforms, including websites and applications. This is accomplished by issuing unique IDs to users, which allows marketers to have a better understanding of how and where their platforms are being visited.

Finally, GA4 may be utilized to provide predictive insights by using a machine-learning method. Marketers may use this powerful new tool to anticipate things like purchase likelihood, activity probability, and revenue predictions.

b. **Mailchimp**

Email campaigns are a critical component of any effective digital marketing plan. Mailchimp is a completely automated email service that allows you to build mailing lists, fully adjustable templates, and fully automated campaigns. Furthermore, Mailchimp provides an analytics solution that may help customers determine the effectiveness of their email marketing plan.

Mailchimp's reporting tools analyze interaction, growth, and income throughout the course of an email campaign, providing users with precise information on what is and isn't working in their plan. Users may also examine how their campaign fared in comparison to rivals. A/B testing enables customers to test several versions of email campaigns and determine which is the most successful method as they go ahead, whilst specialized audience research may provide complete information on consumer groups and demographics.

Not only that, but Mailchimp employs a powerful AI system to provide intelligent recommendations. The technology can create recommendations for product blocks and email content by analyzing over 2 billion data points. MailChimp's AI technology can also offer predictive insights, such as purchase probability data, and it can tag high-value customers with the Customer Lifetime Value tag, enabling marketers to concentrate their efforts on areas where sales are most likely to occur.

Forensiq

Affiliate marketers, for the most part, utilize data to assess their consumers, refine their approach, and produce more conversions. However, data analysis may be used for more than just sales; it can also be used to identify suspicious activity and eliminate the danger of fraud. Fraud may have major consequences, not only affecting financial returns and sales, but also skewing data and making appropriate analysis more difficult. Forensiq is a well-known fraud detection tool.

However, some rookie affiliate marketers may overlook the importance of it for their campaign. Forensiq can examine billions of requests using cutting-edge traffic analysis techniques, passing them through its multi-layered system and alerting any suspicious behavior. Bots, automated devices, and click farms may all be detected as engaging in fraudulent activities.

Users may take use of Forensiq's real-time fraud prevention service, which works by prioritizing interactions and preventing fraudsters. This system learns and streamlines future performance using its own approach. Finally, Forensiq may help advertisers recover reimbursement for losses caused by fraudulent purchases, enabling them to drastically limit the effect of illicit activity.

Monitoring and Evaluating Campaigns

Affiliate marketing is an excellent method of promoting your goods or services online. But how can you know whether your affiliate marketing campaign is effective? How can you know whether your affiliates are influencing sales and conversions? You may use a few important indicators to monitor and analyze your affiliate marketing campaign.

a. **Revenue and conversions**: Sales and conversions are the first and most apparent metrics to monitor. This will show you how much income your affiliate marketing campaign generates.

b. **CTR (click-through rate):** The CTR monitors the number of individuals who click on your affiliate links. A high CTR indicates that your affiliates are effectively marketing your items or services.

c. **AOV (average order value)**: The AOV is the average amount of money spent by customers who buy anything via your affiliate link. A high AOV indicates that your affiliates are bringing in high-value traffic.

d. **CPA (cost per acquisition)**: The CPA is the cost of acquiring a new consumer via your affiliate marketing program. A low cost per acquisition (CPA) indicates that your affiliate marketing campaign is efficient and productive.

Other considerations should be made while monitoring and analyzing your affiliate marketing campaign. First, be sure your expectations are reasonable. Affiliate marketing is not a quick-money scam.

Making it work requires time, effort, and money. Second, don't overlook the cost of goods sold (COGS). This covers the cost of the products or services you're selling, shipping, and any affiliate marketing fees you're paying.

Thirdly, keep in mind that not all sales are made equal. Some affiliates may generate a lot of traffic yet convert at a low rate. Others may have a higher conversion rate but generate fewer visitors. Finding affiliates that provide high-quality traffic that translates into sales and customers is critical.

Fourth, keep an eye on your competitors. What are they doing that is effective? What might you improve on? Keeping an eye on your competitors can help you remain ahead of the game and ensure that your affiliate marketing campaign is as effective as possible.

Finally, don't be hesitant to try new things. Experiment with fresh techniques and evaluate what works best for you and your company. The only way to discover what works is to experiment and see for yourself.

It is critical to monitor and evaluate your affiliate marketing campaign to ensure its effectiveness. You can ensure that your affiliates are generating sales and conversions and that your program is efficient and productive by measuring critical metrics.

Adjusting Strategies for Optimization

A business-focused affiliate must identify their target audience, comprehend their behavior, and develop commerce content that is relevant to their interests. It also necessitates researching SEO best practices, traffic sources, and other elements in order to make affiliate marketing work for you. Including sponsored links in your normal content is a good place to start, but it's just the beginning.

To attain regular, dependable outcomes, you must concentrate on improving your business approach. Here are five pointers to assist you advance your affiliate marketing approach.

a.   Experiment with different merchants.

Most affiliates begin by marketing for a single merchant, generally Amazon or Walmart, since they have an easy-to-understand and execute affiliate scheme. However, these internal initiatives seldom provide the best prices or the most in-demand products. Not to add, when you're tied to a single merchant, any change in their commission rates might completely decimate your cash stream.

Maintaining significant merchant variety ensures that no one vendor has a disproportionate influence on your revenues, and it allows you to alter your approach in reaction to market volatility. You should cast a broad net while selecting merchants.

You should cast a broad net while selecting merchants.

b.   Determine the effectiveness of your plan.

When considering new merchants, it's easy to just target those that pay the most. But keep in mind that the commission rate is simply one part of total success. When analyzing your affiliate marketing performance, use the more complete metric of "earnings per click" (EPC). In addition to commission rate, this measure considers conversion rate and overage order value.

c.   Investigate various affiliate strategies.

As previously said, the opportunities for affiliate profits are nearly endless. You may include affiliate links in a variety of written content, such as product reviews, buyer's guides, and discount sites. You may use affiliate link placements and shoppable photos to leverage social platforms such as YouTube, Twitter, Instagram, Pinterest, and Facebook.

To enhance your editorial material, you may monetise search traffic or develop a curated marketplace. Affiliate marketing provides amazing versatility for all types of publications, so your earning potential is only limited by your ideas. Take some time to experiment with various strategies to find what works best for your specific audience.

d. Investigate various methods of payment.

Traditionally, affiliate marketing is based on commission, with a Cost-Per-Action (CPA) agreement. The affiliate suggests a product, the reader purchases the product from a merchant, and the affiliate earns a commission on the transaction. However, as affiliate marketing expands, new avenues for income emerge.

Cost-Per-Click (CPC) arrangements are becoming more frequent, which implies that the affiliate is paid every time a reader clicks – even if they don't buy anything. Furthermore, Sovrn //Commerce just included real-time bidding (RTB) to CPC campaigns. When a reader clicks on a monetized link, the link is auctioned in real-time, and the reader is led to the merchant via the highest-paying network available.

By using these new forms of monetization, you may increase income while maintaining better control over your revenues.

e. Never underestimate the importance of trust.

One thing is crucial, no matter what kind of content you publish or where you publish it: reader's trust. To earn that trust, you must provide high-quality content that is relevant to your audience. Readers will not react favorably to information that seems to be a direct sales pitch, and they will not appreciate content that is poorly written or presented.

Building confidence among your readers requires authority and sincerity. Once you've established yourself as a trustworthy source, readers will look to you for information as well as purchasing suggestions. While there are several methods to improve your affiliate marketing plan, the most crucial step is to get started.

To begin, select your best-performing content, which might include articles, blog posts, emails, social postings, and more. Then, whenever possible, provide paid links. Pay attention to how your readers react, make changes as required, and develop your affiliate marketing approach in a manner that works best for your audience – and your income objectives.

Chapter 9: Scaling Your Affiliate Marketing Business

"Ambition is the path to success. Persistence is the vehicle you arrive in." — Bill Bradley

Outsourcing and Delegating Tasks

In the realm of affiliate marketing, outsourcing has become a popular and successful method. Affiliate marketers often find themselves juggling several duties, from content production and SEO to campaign management and customer service. You may simplify your marketing efforts by assigning duties like content production, SEO, graphic design, or customer assistance to freelance workers with the necessary skills and experience.

This allows you to concentrate on more important aspects of your company, such as developing strategic relationships, analyzing data, and fine-tuning your marketing tactics. I'd like to discuss how you may outsource simple chores in your affiliate marketing company to simplify your marketing efforts and run a more automated business.

The Advantages of Outsourcing out Affiliate Marketing Tasks

Outsourcing has several advantages that may have a big influence on the profitability and development of your affiliate marketing organization. To begin with, outsourcing enables you to access a pool of specialized talents and knowledge. You may receive high-quality output from specialists who are excellent at what they do by engaging freelancers who are competent in areas where you are weak.

This saves you time since you don't have to put in the effort to achieve the same thing yourself - at the expense of poor quality. Second, outsourcing may result in significant cost reductions. Hiring full-time personnel to handle all aspects of affiliate marketing may be costly, particularly if you're a one-person company.

By outsourcing, you may have access to a flexible workforce while only paying for the services you need. This low-cost method enables you to deploy your money more intelligently, focusing on areas that have a direct influence on revenue production and growth. Finally, outsourcing may considerably boost your affiliate marketing business's scalability.

As your company expands, so will the demands on your time and resources. You may quickly grow your business by outsourcing specific tasks without being weighed down by operational difficulties. This scalability allows you to grasp fresh chances, explore new areas, and vary your marketing efforts without going overboard.

Tips for Outsourcing That Can't Be Ignored

Outsourcing may be a smart choice to help your company grow, save time, and concentrate on core tasks. Here are some tips for properly outsourcing in your affiliate marketing firm.

a. Determine whether tasks should be outsourced

Begin by making a list of all the tasks associated with your affiliate business. Content production, website maintenance, email marketing, social media management, graphic design, SEO, and customer service are all common jobs. Determine which duties you want to outsource depending on your skill level and available time.

b.   Find Trustworthy Outsourcing Partners

Find outsourcing partners or freelancers on reliable sites like as Upwork, Freelancer, Fiverr, or online marketing forums. Examine their profiles, reviews, and ratings to guarantee a respectable track record.

c.   Establish specific instructions and expectations.

Before employing someone, fully describe your project's tasks, responsibilities, and expectations. Create specific instructions and examples to ensure that the outsourcers understand your needs.

d.   Begin Small

If you're dealing with a new freelancer or outsourcing organization, start with a little job to evaluate their abilities and reliability. This will allow you to avoid committing too much money up front before you know whether they are a suitable match.

e.   Communicate Clearly

Keep clear and open lines of communication with your outsourced partners. Stay in contact with them by using project management tools, emails, or communication platforms to offer feedback and clear up any confusion.

f.   Keep Your Data Safe

If your outsourcers require access to sensitive data (e.g., affiliate accounts, website backend), make sure you take the proper security precautions. For further protection, use strong passwords, limit access restrictions, and consider utilizing virtual private networks (VPNs).

g.   Monitor and evaluate performance

Establish key performance indicators (KPIs) to track the effectiveness of your outsourcing operations. Monitor your outsourcers' performance to verify they are meeting your expectations and producing the right outcomes.

h.   Set reasonable deadlines.

Establish clear timelines and give your outsourcers adequate time to perform jobs properly. Rushing might result in poor consequences.

i.   Offer Feedback and Training

Provide positive criticism on a regular basis to assist your outsourcers in improving their job. If necessary, provide further training or tools to help them improve their abilities and comprehension of your affiliate marketing objectives.

j.   Be fair and respectful.

Respect and fairness should be shown to your outsourced partners. Pay them on time and honor their achievements to your company. Outsourcing is an iterative process that requires some trial and error. Because not every freelancer or outsourcing partner will be a great match for your affiliate marketing firm, be prepared to make modifications as required.

Outsourcing Options for Your Affiliate Business

We recently discussed the advantages of outsourcing, and I provided you some pointers on what to do when delegating sections of your company to freelancers. Now I'd like to provide you a list of some of the products in your affiliate marketing business that can be outsourced.

Here are a few examples of typical chores that may be outsourced:

a.   Making Content

Any effective affiliate marketing strategy is built on content. Engaging, useful, and SEO-optimized content attracts organic traffic, builds audience trust, and drives conversions. Creating high-quality content on a continuous basis, on the other hand, may be a difficult endeavor, particularly when you need to concentrate on other elements of your organization.

Outsourcing content production to expert writers, bloggers, or content companies may help you maintain a consistent supply of intriguing articles, blog posts, product reviews, and social media content. Provide specific rules and create the tone of voice you want when outsourcing article development. Review the material on a regular basis to verify that it is consistent with your brand image and marketing goals.

Encourage your content writers to perform extensive research and deliver important insights to your audience, which will increase engagement and position you as an authority person in your area.

b.   Search Engine Optimization (SEO)

If you want to rank higher in search engine results and boost your chances of converting visitors into customers, you must have a well-optimized website. However, SEO is a difficult and ever-changing area that needs ongoing efforts and knowledge. Outsourcing your SEO responsibilities to experts may transform your affiliate marketing business.

SEO professionals may do extensive keyword research, assess competition, optimize on-page features, develop high-quality backlinks, and boost website speed and performance. Furthermore, they can maintain track on algorithm upgrades and make the appropriate changes to keep your website ahead of the competition. By outsourcing SEO, you can concentrate on other strategic elements of your organization while ensuring that your website stays search engine friendly and competitive.

c.   Multimedia and graphic design

Visually attractive content increases audience engagement and conversions significantly. Graphic design and multimedia play an important part in affiliate marketing, from eye-catching landing sites to intriguing infographics and video material. However, you may lack the creative abilities or software knowledge required to generate great images. Outsourcing graphic design and multimedia work to expert designers and video editors may improve the overall look and feel of your marketing contents.

It may also assist you in delivering a consistent brand identity across several channels, so confirming your reputation and authority in the niche.

d. Email Promotion

Email marketing is still one of the most efficient methods for nurturing leads, generating recurring business, and promoting affiliate products. Managing email campaigns, developing compelling newsletters, and guaranteeing timely delivery, on the other hand, may be time-consuming and resource-intensive. You may harness the experience of specialists who know the best practices for producing captivating email text, building visually attractive templates, and maximizing deliverability by outsourcing email marketing activities.

Furthermore, professional email marketers can examine success indicators like open rates, click-through rates, and conversion rates to help you fine-tune your email marketing approach for better outcomes. They may also help you establish email lists that will increase the conversion rates of your affiliate products.

e. Social Media Administration

You may use social media sites to engage with your target audience, establish a devoted following, and generate traffic to your affiliate site. Managing many social media accounts, creating interesting posts, and replying to comments and messages, on the other hand, may be daunting. Outsourcing social media management to specialists enables you to keep an active presence on social media platforms without being overburdened. Skilled social media managers can help you enhance your social media strategy by creating a content calendar, scheduling posts, engaging with followers, and analyzing performance indicators.

f. Website Development and Upkeep

A well-designed and user-friendly website is essential for your affiliate marketing business's success. You can guarantee that your website is visually beautiful, mobile-responsive, and conversion-optimized by outsourcing website creation and maintenance responsibilities to expert web developers. Web developers may also improve the security, speed, and general performance of your website, resulting in a seamless and delightful user experience for your audience.

g. Management of Paid Advertising

Paid advertising, such as Google advertisements or social network advertisements, may be a powerful tool for directing focused traffic to your affiliate offerings. Paid advertising efforts, on the other hand, need continual monitoring, optimization, and budget management. Outsourcing paid advertising management to PPC (Pay-Per-Click) professionals may assist you in maximizing the effectiveness of various advertising channels.

These professionals can do keyword research, write persuasive ad text, set up and optimize campaigns, and offer regular performance reports. You can make data-driven choices, optimize your ad budget, and get a greater return on investment (ROI) with their help.

h. Analysis and reporting of data

Understanding your affiliate marketing performance is essential for fine-tuning your strategy and increasing income. Outsourcing data analysis and reporting activities to analysts or data professionals might help you save time and get useful insights. These professionals can spot patterns, monitor key performance indicators (KPIs), and find opportunities for development.

You can make educated judgments to maximize your affiliate marketing efforts and content strategy if you have data-driven insights.

i. Customer Service

Excellent customer service is critical for guaranteeing customer satisfaction and loyalty. Responding to queries and resolving difficulties, on the other hand, may be time-consuming and may not be viable if you have a small staff or work as a solopreneur. Outsourcing customer service to dedicated specialists or support teams helps guarantee that your customers get timely and effective assistance.

These professionals can manage typical questions, fix technological difficulties, and give quick remedies, improving your affiliate marketing business's overall client experience and reputation.

j.   Production of Video

You may outsource video production and editing if you perform Youtube marketing and want to integrate video content in your affiliate marketing plan. You may assure that your videos are of the greatest quality by outsourcing video creation to skilled videographers or production firms. Professional videographers have the skills, equipment, and ability to produce visually attractive and engaging videos that complement your brand image and marketing objectives.

Video creation may be a time-consuming and resource-intensive procedure, particularly if you are unfamiliar with video editing and production. Outsourcing this process helps you to concentrate on other important areas of your affiliate marketing company, such as content development, email marketing, and developing new sales funnels.

Final Thoughts on Affiliate Marketing Outsourcing

Outsourcing certain areas of your affiliate marketing company may provide various benefits, including higher productivity, access to specialized knowledge, and the potential to expand your organization more effectively. You may develop a more efficient and effective company model by assigning specific tasks to trusted outsourcing partners, leading to long-term success in affiliate marketing. You can concentrate on automating your company, increasing revenue growth, and keeping ahead of your competitors online via strategic outsourcing.

Expanding Your Product Portfolio and Diversifying Income Streams

The saying "don't put all your eggs in one basket" bears great truth in the dynamic world of affiliate marketing. As astute affiliate marketers, I recognize that depending only on a single income source may be dangerous. In this section, we will delve into the art of diversity in affiliate marketing, revealing tactics, advantages, and the way to increasing your revenue potential.

Let's take a look at the world of varied affiliate marketing portfolios, where opportunity meets innovation.

Recognizing the Importance of Diversification

At its essence, affiliate marketing is promoting products or services and receiving commissions for each sale or action generated by your marketing efforts. While this base is unwavering, it is critical to note that the channels via which these revenues might be earned are as varied as the digital world itself.

Investigating Different Revenue Streams

a. **Content Diversity**: Investing in several forms of content will help you reach and engage a larger audience. To respond to varied learning and consumption habits, combine written blogs, interesting videos, infographics, and even podcasts.

b. **Affiliate Marketing**: Explore affiliate programs outside of your comfort zone. While product-based programs are prevalent, think about branching out into software, online courses, subscription services, and other areas. This diversification might introduce you to new areas and sectors.

c. **Email Marketing**: Developing a strong email marketing plan may be game-changing. Emails may lead to substantial conversions by doing anything from creating a devoted subscriber list to offering important insights and special offers.

d. **Social Media Engagement**: Potential consumers congregate in large numbers on social media channels. From Instagram to Twitter, use these networks to artistically exhibit your affiliate items and communicate with your audience.

e. **Webinars and Workshops**: Hosting webinars or workshops might help you establish yourself as an expert in your field. These events allow opportunity to educate, interact, and incorporate affiliate marketing smoothly.

The Advantages of Diversification

a. **Risk Mitigation**: By diversifying your income sources, you protect yourself from the volatility that may develop if one stream underperforms. A drop in one area might be offset by growth in another.

b. **Broader Audience Reach**: Different kinds of content and platforms appeal to different audiences. Diversification helps you to reach a greater range of prospective clients.

c. **Increased reputation**: A diverse portfolio will help you gain reputation as an affiliate marketer. By demonstrating skill in several areas, you establish oneself as a diverse and informed authority.

d. **Trend Adaptability**: The digital world is always changing, with new trends coming and vanishing. A diverse strategy allows you to quickly adjust to changes and capitalize on new trends.

Taking the Diversification Road

a. **Investigation and analysis**: Diversification is built on thorough study and analysis. To adapt your approach, learn about your audience's preferences, pain areas, and habits.

b. **Strategy Planning**: Create a strategy plan outlining the many income sources you want to pursue. Allocate resources and time wisely to ensure that each stream gets sufficient attention.

c. **Consistency**: In all fields, consistency is essential. Maintain a consistent brand voice, appearance, and messaging to provide your audience with a consistent experience.

d. **Data-Driven Optimization**: Monitor and assess the performance of each income stream on a continuous basis. Use data insights to improve your plans and maximize their efficacy.

Conclusion: A Range of Possibilities

As we come to the end of our voyage through the world of diverse affiliate marketing portfolios, keep in mind that each income stream offers a distinct possibility. You may increase your earning potential by embracing variety, being adaptive, and always improving your techniques. So, take the risk, experiment, and create a web of cash streams that correspond to your skills, hobbies, and target audience.

Chapter 10: Overcoming Challenges

"Selling to people through social media is like going to a party, meeting somebody for the first time, and then saying, 'Hey, do you want to buy this Tupperware?'" – Pat Flynn

Dealing with Rejection and Setbacks

Rejection is painful, whether it comes from a consumer, a friend, or a love relationship. You cannot, as an entrepreneur, turn a blind eye to client rejection. It not only hurts emotionally, but it also poses a serious danger to the success of your company.

Startups are particularly vulnerable: according to a recent study, over 90% of startups fail during the first ten years.

One of the most common reasons for failure?

Customer Rejection.

Every business has difficulties. However, it might be tough when your livelihood is at stake and you've just recently opened your doors.

What Exactly Is Customer Rejection?

The brief definition of customer rejection is self-explanatory. It occurs when customers reject your products or services. However, it is critical to understand when and where this description applies. Rejection may indicate that your product or service is not in demand, that there are other businesses that match customers' demands, that your products/services are of poor quality or are costly, or that you are simply not reaching customers.

The First Reaction

Your first response to rejection may not be the most beneficial, particularly if you are new to the startup "community." Rejection of your company might seem like the end of the world at first; a personal assault on your character and a signal to give up. This is a normal response, but it is ultimately counterproductive.

Although 90% of small companies fail, quitting up too soon means that you will not be among the 10% who succeed. It might be difficult to maintain objectivity in the face of rejection.

However, in order for your business to thrive, you must learn how to deal with it constructively. One of the reasons so many businesses fail is a lack of demand for their products. If this is the case with your businesses, you must learn how to change your methods and your connection with your target market while refusing to give up.

First Steps in Dealing with Rejection Constructively

Customer rejection may be used to help your startup or company develop in a variety of ways. When dealing with customers, marketers usually use a number of strategies to deal with rejection. The first pain is unavoidable, but it might help you discover new and better sales tactics.

Learning how to cope with rejection involves work on all levels: emotionally, psychologically, and practically. Fortunately, we have some pointers that may help you change your attitude regarding consumer rejection.

a. Try not to take it personally.

It's much easier said than done. Customer rejection is unpleasant, but it is an unavoidable aspect of being an entrepreneur. Customer rejection may take many different forms, some gentler than others, but most of us are conditioned to take criticism personally.

Many individuals grow up valuing themselves based on their accomplishments—academic or sports success, or any other endeavor that earned them praise from their parents or other authority figures. It's difficult to unlearn that way of thinking, but every great entrepreneur has had to change their attitude toward praise and rejection first. Rejection is about your company, not your personality, and you can't afford to react to it with your ego.

b. Modify your mentality

Changing one's attitude begins with not taking customer rejection personally. You may not have a "attitude problem" per se, but changing your mentality is an important element of developing as an entrepreneur and surviving rejection. Aside from avoiding taking customer rejection personally, there are a variety of activities you may do to shift your mindset about rejection from despair to resolve.

Adopting a growth mentality may help you see every sales contact, email, or discussion as a chance to develop. One of them is self-education. Every entrepreneur will confront some kind of rejection.

This has happened to some of the greatest names in industry. A substantial majority of businesses fail, but even those that do thrive have experienced challenges. It's not the rejection itself that hurts, but what you do with it: identifying and resolving the fundamental problem.

c. Take notes

The desire to study is one of the cornerstones to success in any area. Being teachable and open-minded may bring you farther than you realize. The first step is to determine why your business/product/service was rejected and if you can do something about it.

If you haven't previously, get feedback from your customer, particularly addressing any apparent deficit. This may be done in person or online and is really beneficial in getting you back on track. It's possible that your product/service is in tremendous demand, but your technique to marketing it has failed.

Make no mistake: some rejections are based on unfulfilled customer demands, but not all. Marketing, for example, is something that many businesses deal with—and sometimes struggle with. Self-promotion is not inexpensive, but it is necessary.

If you get a significant rejection, it is conceivable that your marketing approach, rather than your product/service, is flawed. Listening is also an important part of growing after rejection. Seeking input from your target market is pointless unless you are willing to listen to and comprehend it.

It's natural to want to lick your (metaphorical) wounds. However, communicating with your detractors is more effective in the long term.

d.   Address the problems

Marketing success involves both persuading abilities and the perseverance to deal with the numerous NOs. When faced with customer rejection, entrepreneurs may respond in one of two ways: destructively or constructively. After receiving criticism and giving yourself a pep talk, it's time to address the underlying problems, i.e., what you can do to get beyond this kind of setback.

Practical Advice on Using Rejection to Grow

Things start to become serious at this stage. It's one thing to get your mind around customer rejection. However, tackling it practically requires specific action and specialized solutions.

a.   Get rid of anything you don't want.

Customer rejection is caused by buyers who do not desire what is being supplied to them. If this is your product or service, it is time to rethink your startup. Did you do the essential market research to determine if there is a demand for what you're selling?

If you made a mistake, attempt to figure out if you need to ditch your concept entirely or if there are changes you can make that will capture the attention of your target market.

b.   **Think about your connection with your target market.**

If you are experiencing customer rejection but know that there is a need for your products/services, you might reconsider how you interact with your target market. One of the pillars of entrepreneurship is marketing. It is not a simple task, but it is a crucial aspect of business that may make or ruin your firm.

Getting your business off the ground is dependent on a variety of factors. You'll need excellent branding, an identity, marketing objectives, creating relationships with customers, and knowing which marketing channels to prioritize.

c.   **Determine the finest marketing plan for your company.**

Startups often lack the resources to fund large marketing initiatives, yet it is still feasible to get a decent ROI. If you need to do further market research after being rejected, consider the unmet demands of your clients. Customers may reject items or services simply because they lack sufficient knowledge about them, which is where smart marketing comes into play.

One of the most effective methods to overcome rejection in sales is to concentrate on the next opportunity. Salespeople who have a large amount of activity in their pipeline are less likely to get disheartened by each rejection. Social media provides several chances to promote your brand, both via your own page and through sponsored adverts, and a skilled marketing professional will be able to determine which kind of campaign works best.

Aside from social media marketing, entrepreneurs must have good branding, open lines of contact with customers, eye-catching online content (including excellent SEO), and a regular presence in their niche.

d.   **Reassess on a regular basis**

Rejection is a part of the sales process that everyone goes through. Don't be afraid to rethink your sales plan on a frequent basis. When you're buried in the day-to-day grind of operating a business, it's easy to lose sight of the broader picture.

You may feel even more pressure to buckle down and work harder after a rejection. However, if you want to support quick company development, you must do frequent business assessments. Picking yourself up after a customer rejection takes time, just like the rejection itself.

When you assess things often, you are more likely to see trends and warning indicators, allowing you to change your approach.

Growth Takes Time

Sales rejection is unavoidable, and let's be honest, it's frequently painful. But there's no need to panic: rejection is a natural outcome of our capacity to learn, adapt, and evolve. As the sales rejections mount up, you start to wonder whether it's an indication that you're growing worse or if there's something fundamentally wrong with your personality.

If this is occurring, consider times when your expertise helped a prospect. Maintain a professional manner: Remaining cool and thankful amid rejection will help you convey a good tone to costumers.

Remaining cool and thankful amid rejection will help you convey a good tone to costumers.

This might increase your company's reputation and raise the chances of future business with the customer. Entrepreneurship is not for the faint of heart. According to research, about 80% of small enterprises in the United States have just one employee: the founder. The majority of them are reliant on personal savings. Starting a company entails several dangers, one of which is customer rejection.

However, if you already know how to manage this, you're one step ahead.

Staying Motivated in the Affiliate Marketing Journey

Affiliate marketing is a competitive business that takes effort, ingenuity, and passion to thrive. Staying motivated as an affiliate marketer is critical for sustaining constant efforts and establishing long-term success. You will confront obstacles and challenges that will put your strength and determination to thrive in this field to the test.

If you want to excel in affiliate marketing, you must have the strength to keep pushing.

Why You Should Be Motivated As An Affiliate

Staying inspired is more than a passing wish; it is a key need for success in affiliate marketing. Motivation gives the continual drive needed to negotiate the complex web of hurdles that affiliate marketers often face. These roadblocks may be frustrating, ranging from changes in SEO algorithm to variations in customer behavior.

A motivated mentality, on the other hand, will enable you to face these obstacles with a problem-solving perspective, converting failures into stepping stones toward progress. The road of affiliate marketing is one of constant learning and change. With technology and trends changing so quickly, you must remain up to date on the newest techniques and tools.

Motivation is the driving force behind this continuing education. It piques your interest in trying out new strategies, experimenting with new platforms, and being open to new ways to improve your marketing strategy. Without drive, complacency in using obsolete ways may stymie your growth and restrict your accomplishment.

Furthermore, in affiliate marketing, motivation is the foundation of resilience. The road to success is not straightforward. Along the process, there will be highs and lows.

A driven affiliate marketer is better able to withstand disappointment and losses. Rather than being disappointed by a campaign that does not provide instant results, redirect your energy into assessing the problem, discovering areas for improvement, and changing your techniques for future initiatives. As an associate, being motivated adds to a stronger work-life balance and general well-being.

Affiliate marketing may be very time-consuming, blurring the distinction between business and leisure time. Staying motivated increases your chances of setting limits, prioritizing self-care, and avoiding burnout. You may continue your love and excitement for affiliate marketing over time if you keep motivated, leading to a more rewarding, gratifying, and successful career path.

Keep These Motivational Affiliate Marketing Tips in Mind

Let's talk about some techniques to keep motivated in your affiliate marketing journey now that you know why it's vital. These suggestions must be implemented, but they are really easy and practical, requiring just your time, heart, and head.

The first tip for keeping motivated as an affiliate marketer is as follows:

a.   Establish Specific Objectives

Purpose is essential for staying motivated in affiliate marketing. Setting specific and attainable objectives gives you the direction and concentration you need to drive your efforts. Define short-term and long-term goals, such as monthly sales targets, website traffic targets, or special affiliate product promotions.

Breaking down major objectives into smaller, practical tasks can give you a feeling of success with each milestone reached, increasing your motivation along the way.

b.   Imagine Success

Many successful affiliate marketers employ visualization as a key tactic. Spend a few minutes each day visualizing yourself reaching your objectives. Consider the thrill of your first affiliate sale, the pleasure of expanding your revenue, or the satisfaction of a well-executed marketing campaign. Visualizing achievement strengthens your commitment and keeps your drive strong.

c.   Stay Informed and Educated

The affiliate marketing business is always changing, with new trends, tools, and techniques appearing all the time. Invest time in constant learning to remain motivated. Attend webinars, read industry blogs, and follow industry thought leaders.

The more you learn, the more confident and determined you will be to execute new ideas and respond to market developments.

d. Develop a Positive Attitude

A good outlook is essential for motivation. Believe in your abilities to overcome obstacles and accomplish your objectives. Accept setbacks as learning opportunities rather than obstacles. Engage in helpful affiliate marketing forums, read inspiring literature, and practice mindfulness techniques to surround oneself with positivity. A good attitude will keep you energetic and ready to face any challenges that may arise

e. Establish a Productive Workplace

Your working environment has a big influence on your motivation and productivity. Make your workstation pleasant, orderly, and favorable to creative. Make it your own by adding motivating words, images of your aspirations, and aspects that encourage you. A well-organized office will help you stay focused and motivated throughout your affiliate marketing journey.

f. Rejoice in Small Victories

Don't wait for great accomplishments to be celebrated. Recognize and appreciate every minor victory you earn along the road. Whether it's a successful email campaign, a blog comment on your affiliate site, or reaching a particular amount of social media followers, these triumphs legitimize your efforts and motivate you to keep going.

g. Network with Other Marketers

Affiliate marketing may be isolated at times, but engaging with other marketers can create a feeling of community and drive. Participate in online forums, social media groups, and networking events to share ideas, experiences, and tips. Participating in a community of like-minded people may bring vital insights, fresh energy, and a reminder that you are not alone on your path.

h. Use a Content Calendar to Stay Organized

In affiliate marketing, consistency is essential. A content calendar aids in the planning and organization of your marketing operations, providing a consistent flow of content and promotions. Having a clear roadmap of what needs to be done and when will help you avoid overwhelm and procrastination while also keeping you motivated by demonstrating progress and success.

i. **Give Yourself a Treat**

Reward yourself for achieving milestones and objectives. Set up a reward system that corresponds to your accomplishments. Whether it's a favorite treat, a day off, or investing in a new business tool, incentives reinforce great behavior and give a practical motivation to remain engaged.

j. **Accept Adaptability**

At times, affiliate marketing may be unexpected, with methods that work one day becoming outdated the next. Accept flexibility as a basic feature. Be willing to change, try new techniques, and learn from mistakes.

This adaptability not only keeps your affiliate marketing efforts current, but it also keeps you engaged and driven by the thrill of innovation. Motivation is the driving force that leads affiliate marketers to success. You may create an atmosphere of constant inspiration by defining clear objectives, envisioning accomplishment, having a good mentality, and remaining informed.

Remember that versatility is an asset in affiliate marketing. By adding these ten effective motivating principles into your affiliate marketing journey, you'll be better prepared to overcome obstacles and accomplish extraordinary achievements. Take these suggestions and implement them into your attitude now to attain heights of success you never imagined possible.

Best wishes on your affiliate marketing adventure!

Learning from Mistakes

Affiliate marketing is a popular method to earn money online, but it is also a competitive business fraught with risks. Here are some typical pitfalls to avoid while beginning your affiliate marketing journey in order to increase your chances of success:

a. **Choosing the incorrect products**: One of the most common errors novices make is selecting products that are not relevant to their niche or audience. Select products that are both relevant to your specialty and in great demand. Look for products that provide large commissions and regular cash flow.

b. **Failure to provide value**: Affiliate marketing is more than simply advertising items; it is also about giving value to your audience. Create meaningful content that addresses your audience's pain points. To engage your audience, use a variety of content forms such as blog entries, videos, and social media updates.

c. **Overpromoting**: By bombarding your audience with promotional offers, you risk alienating them and jeopardizing your trust. Balance your promotional material with useful information that solves your audience's needs.

d. **Ignoring SEO**: Search engine optimization (SEO) is a very effective method for driving organic traffic to your affiliate marketing content. Improve your search engine ranks by optimizing your content for relevant keywords, meta tags, and descriptions.

e. **Affiliate links must be disclosed**: The Federal Trade Commission (FTC) requires affiliates to disclose their affiliate links. Failure to disclose your affiliate links might harm your reputation and potentially lead to legal action.

f. **Creating an email list** is vital for creating connections with your audience and promoting your affiliate items. To develop your email list, provide lead magnets like as e-books, webinars, and free trials. Send out periodical mailings with useful information and promotional offers.

g. **Choosing the incorrect affiliate program**: Not all affiliate programs are the same. Select affiliate programs with a solid reputation, substantial commission rates, and excellent customer service. Avoid programs that have a reputation of underpaying affiliates or providing bad customer support.

To summarize, affiliate marketing may be a successful method to generate money online, but it takes time and work. To increase your chances of success, avoid these typical blunders while beginning your affiliate marketing adventure. Select the appropriate products, add value, balance your content, optimize for SEO, reveal your affiliate links, establish an email list, and select the appropriate affiliate programs.

Follow these pointers to succeed in the cutthroat world of affiliate marketing.

a. Prioritizing Selling Over Assistance

As an internet marketer, it's easy to get into the attitude that obtaining conversions/sales is your first objective. Unfortunately, it is this thinking that leads to substandard material and bad outcomes. Instead, prioritize providing high-value content above anything else. Concentrate your writing on the reader's intention, putting them first. Instead of describing features, concentrate on the user's benefits.

Wherever possible, avoid user friction. Banner advertising have their uses, but are they worth annoying your visitors to the point of abandonment? Will Google consider your pop-ups to be invasive content?

Every outbound sales strategy, whether a banner ad or a notification request, has ramifications. You must determine if the user friction is worthwhile.

b. Creating Low-Quality Content

As an affiliate marketer, whether you like it or not, your content is your product. Clicks are merely the outcome of quality content that people value and trust. Affiliate marketers should prioritize the creation of high-quality content above all else. Far too many affiliates believe that ten poor posts will outperform one outstanding one.

This is not true. When it comes to writing high-quality blog entries in order to outrank the competition in the SERPs, there are a few measures to remember. The first step is to pick a topic that can be ranked for, sometimes known as "low hanging fruit."

After you've determined the topic, do keyword research to determine what it will take to outrank the competitors.

Consider the following:

How many backlinks to the root domain do they have? To find out how many backlinks the competition has, use a tool like **MozBar**. What is the word count of the most popular posts? The typical first-page result is 1,890 words long.

When creating your own content, keep this duration in mind as a basic guideline. Is there a picture in your post? According to research, posts featuring at least one picture rank better than those without. How is the post's readability?

You'll have the structure you need to develop a top-ranking piece of content after you've unearthed these information. After that, devote as much effort to advertising your freshly released content as you did to writing it:

- Use social media to promote your new guide.
- Send it to your mailing list.
- Reach out to relevant blogs to urge them to link back to your guide.

c.   Ignoring/Ignoring Site Speed

Did you know that if your web page takes more than 2 seconds to load, your bounce rate increases by 50%? We are all aware that customers are impatient. If your site's speed makes users wait, they won't, and your bounce rate will suffer as a result.

Visit GTMetrix.com for a breakdown of what could be causing your site to load slowly. A sluggish site is usually caused by slow server response times, big files, or a poor method of content distribution. If you're using WordPress, there are a few plugins that I can suggest time and time again.

- **Imagify**: If huge photographs are a problem, utilize Imagify to compress them as much as feasible without compromising quality.

- **WP Rocket**: For content delivery, we suggest enabling browser caching and experimenting with delaying CSS and JavaScript rendering using WP Rocket. A word of caution: changing the JavaScript and CSS rendering might create difficulties with your website's functioning, therefore we suggest contacting your development team or an SEO professional for assistance.

- **CDN Cloudflare**: When in doubt, use the Cloudflare WordPress plugin to install a CDN to speed up content delivery.

- **Contact the Convertly team for Shopify sites**. They provide comparable site performance optimization services for Shopify sites.

Although not every site will load in under 2 seconds, there are steps you can do to increase your site's performance. Not only will faster load times improve user experience, but they will also improve rankings and conversion rates.

d. Neglecting Content Readability

Visitors have a lesser tolerance for complicated or difficult-to-read material in this day and age of shorter attention spans. When it comes to font size, any type less than 16pt should be avoided, especially for mobile users. However, font size isn't the primary consideration for readability.

In your blog themes, you should also consider line height, serif versus sans fonts, and tracking. When in doubt, the age-old "rule of thumb" for paragraph writing is to choose a serif font. Try to avoid using extended phrases and paragraphs.

According to studies, beyond 25 words, a phrase gets difficult to read. The same logic applies to paragraphs, which should be limited to four sentences or fewer wherever feasible. If you have to search up a word to utilize it in your work, leave it out.

According to studies, readers in the United States prefer a reading level of seventh to eighth grade. This also applies to readers with a higher academic level. Before you click the publish button, check Hemingway to see how your contented is rated.

e. Lack of a thorough understanding of what you're selling

One of the most frequent errors we see affiliate marketers make is failing to devote the time necessary to learn about the subject matter of their articles. Don't underestimate your readers' intelligence. With access to all of the world's knowledge at their fingertips, prospective customer will be ready to call your bluff if you don't know what you're talking about. So, how do you deal with this?

Stay up to speed on your topic by subscribing to industry-leading blogs, forums, or Google alerts. Go to Quora or Reddit to see what questions people have regarding your topic. Above all, arm yourself with the information required to gain your readers' trust and involvement via your content.

This will benefit in the long run, both in terms of conversions and page engagement in Google's eyes.

f. Ignoring SEO Fundamentals

Publishing a new content without good SEO is like constructing a home without any roads leading to it. Without the right title tag and meta description, readers will have a tough, if not impossible, time finding your content. After all, you're in the business of producing as much traffic as possible, right? The first step is to improve your meta description and title tag.

Investigate your post's underlying concept and aim to build an engaging title tag and meta description for possible visitors. Consider this your sales presentation in search engine results.

The visitor is more likely to click through to your website if your title tag and meta description connect with them.

If you have a WordPress website, you may do this by using the Yoast SEO Plugin. Then you must concentrate on generating interesting material for your meta description and title tag. Otherwise, we suggest contacting an SEO specialist for assistance.

External and internal relationships should not be overlooked. Internal links contribute to the site's information structure and link equity. External links are seen to be the most essential source of ranking power. External links are the most effective technique for Google to determine the trustworthiness and authority of another site's content.

Skim over your message, looking for chances to connect to other pages on your site.

g.   Not Making Use of Evergreen Content

The internet evolves quickly, and it is our responsibility as content creators to stay up. Articles like "The Best "X" of 2025" are important in web marketing. You should, however, balance this material with long-term, evergreen content. Especially in terms of long-term link building value.

For those who are unfamiliar, consider it a content that receives a regular amount of search queries throughout the year and over a lengthy period of time. As you may expect, evergreen content is often a far more competitive field. Because other successful bloggers and content marketers understand the long-term worth, competing in this field may be challenging.

It is also said that evergreen content is less beneficial for affiliates since much of it is prepared in the form of "how-tos" and instructional manuals. While this argument has some merit, there is still a tremendous amount of link building value to be gained by generating long-form sustainable content. To address this, use elements such as [2023 Edition] or (Updated for 2023) in the post title to raise the value of your content even more.

Examine your content approach again. Are you primarily writing specialized and timely content? If this is the case, try creating some Awareness Content that will continue to create link value for years to come.

Conclusion

Recap of Key Concepts

As we conclude the book on this comprehensive journey through affiliate marketing, let's go over the key ideas that have served as the foundation of your newly gained knowledge.

1. Understanding Affiliate Marketing

   - Recognize the core principles and historical evolution of affiliate marketing.

   - Looked at its critical role in the ever-changing digital ecology.

2. Setting Realistic Goals

- Set defined, measurable, and reachable goals to guide your affiliate marketing journey.

   - Recognized the transformative power of goal-setting for long-term success.

3. Building Your Foundation

- Identified a profitable niche and target audiences.

  - Made informed choices regarding the affiliate products you promote.

4. Crafting Your Online Presence

- Established a strong online presence by developing an exceptional website or blog.

- Integration of social media platforms and search engine optimization.

5. Crafting Compelling Content

- Acknowledged the importance of quality content in engaging your audience.

  - Discovered how to produce effective product reviews and intriguing blog posts.

6. Mastering the Art of Promotion

- Employed a number of promotional methods, such as email marketing, social media, and paid advertising.

  - Investigated methods to widen your reach and maximize the impact of your marketing.

7. Understanding Affiliate Networks

- Successfully navigated the affiliate network ecosystem, selecting programs intelligently.

  - Increased income via wise judgments made inside these networks.

8. Analyzing and Improving Performance

- Explored analytics technologies for campaign performance monitoring and assessment.

- Changed approaches for ongoing optimization and improvement.

9. Scaling Your Affiliate Marketing Business

- Looked at opportunities for expanding your business, such as outsourcing and diversifying income streams.

  - Discovered how to diversify your product portfolio for long-term growth.

10. Overcoming Challenges

These key concepts will serve as your guideposts as you begin your affiliate marketing journey. May your path be filled with constant learning, advancement, and the fulfillment of your ambitions. Best luck for your adventures in the exciting world of affiliate marketing!

Encouragement to Continued Success

As you near the conclusion of your affiliate marketing journey, keep in mind that it will be a continual process. In the ever-changing digital world, success is a journey rather than a destination. Here's a powerful message of encouragement to keep you going:

1. Accept the Learning Journey: Affiliate marketing is an ever-changing business. Accept the learning road with passion, realizing that each challenge is an opportunity to grow.

2. Persistence is Required: Success is seldom attained overnight. Continue to be persistent, fine-tune your tactics, and keep in mind that the journey is just as important as the destination.

3. Mark Significant and Minor Milestones: Recognize and celebrate your achievements, whether they be financial milestones or the successful execution of a new marketing strategy.

4. Maintain Adaptability in a Changing Environment: The digital landscape is always changing. Be adaptable, open to new ideas, and flexible in your approach to navigating the twists and turns.

5. Network and Collaborate: Make connections with other affiliate marketers, join organizations, and work on relevant initiatives together. The insights and support of a community may be critical.

6. Reframe Difficulties as Opportunities: Every route has challenges. Reframe difficulties as opportunities for development and creativity. Every difficulty is a chance to learn and enhance your plan.

7. Put your Health First. Profit is not the sole metric of success. Make your mental and physical well-being a priority in order to sustain the energy essential for long-term success.

8. Review and Refine Goals: Your goals should evolve with you. Revisit and change your objectives on a frequent basis to keep up with your expanding ambitions and the changing affiliate marketing landscape.

9. Create a Positive Attitude: Create a positive and resilient mindset. Your attitude toward challenges has a significant impact on your ability to overcome them.

10. Enjoy the View: Don't forget to take in the scenery in the midst of the strategies, statistics, and marketing. Celebrate the little victories, enjoy the learning opportunities, and enjoy the trip.

Keep in mind that success is a series of milestones on a dynamic journey, not a single destination, as you go, inspired by knowledge and effort. May your affiliate marketing journey be one of ongoing improvement, fulfillment, and realization of your goals. Best regards!

Your Next Steps in Affiliate Marketing

Congratulations on reaching this pivotal point in your affiliate marketing career! As you stand armed with knowledge, goals, and a clear strategy, the following steps are important in propelling you toward success. Here is a checklist to assist you in planning your next steps in your exciting adventure:

1. **Implementation and Iteration**: Act on the concepts from this crash course straight away. Put the strategies into action, and be prepared to iterate based on real-world results.

2. **Be a part of Affiliate Marketing Communities**: Participate in online communities, forums, and social media groups to meet other affiliate marketers. Share your experiences, get advice, and benefit from the collective knowledge of the community.

3. **Stay Up to Date on Industry Trends**: The digital landscape is ever-changing. Maintain current knowledge of market trends, new technologies, and changes in client behavior so that you can alter your strategies accordingly.

4. **Vary Your Income Streams**: Look for other ways to vary your money streams. Consider new subjects, products, or affiliate programs that will compliment your existing abilities and target audience.

5. **Invest in Ongoing Education**: Affiliate marketing is a fast-paced business. Invest in your continued education by reading industry blogs, attending webinars, and researching advanced courses.

6. **Performance Monitoring and Analysis**: Regularly monitor the performance of your campaigns. Use analytics tools to monitor important indicators, review data, and make smart decisions to optimize your strategy.

7. **Set New Goals and Challenges**: When you achieve your previous goals, set new ones. Scale your business, explore new areas, or try out new marketing methods to propel yourself to new heights.

8. **Network and Collaborate**: Make important contacts among affiliate marketers. Collaborations, partnerships, and shared ideas may result from networking, all of which may help you succeed.

9. **Consider Scaling Your Business**: Look for strategies to grow your affiliate marketing business. Consider outsourcing work, increasing your personnel, and expanding your advertising operations to reach a bigger audience.

10. **Enjoy the Fruits of Your Labor**: Celebrate your successes along the way. Take some time to reflect on how far you've come, to acknowledge your achievements, and to enjoy the fruits of your labor.

Remember that your affiliate marketing journey is dynamic and ever-changing. Approach it with energy, adaptability, and a desire to embrace fresh opportunities. As you continue through the next phases, may your trip be marked by steady development, satisfaction, and the fulfillment of your affiliate marketing goals. Have a great day exploring!

Appendix

Resources and Tools

Your affiliate marketing journey is aided by a multitude of information and tools that may help you improve your abilities, simplify your operations, and stay up to date on industry trends. Here's a list of resources to help you succeed in the long run:

Online Courses and Training Platforms

1. Udemy (https://www.udemy.com/) - Examine a range of affiliate marketing courses for people of all skill levels.

2. Coursera (https://www.coursera.org/) - Learn about digital marketing and affiliate tactics from renowned institutions.

3. HubSpot Academy (https://academy.hubspot.com/) - Free online courses on a variety of digital marketing subjects.

Blogs and Websites

1. Affiliate Summit (https://www.affiliatesummit.com/blog/) - Keep up with industry news, insights, and expert viewpoints.

2. Neil Patel (https://neilpatel.com/blog/) - Neil Patel's blog contains in-depth advice on numerous facets of digital marketing, including affiliate marketing.

3. Smart Passive Income (https://www.smartpassiveincome.com/) - Pat Flynn discusses his thoughts and ideas for generating passive income.

Affiliate Marketing Tools

1. Analytics:

- Google Analytics (https://analytics.google.com/) - Analyze and track website traffic and user activity.

- Clicky (https://clicky.com/) - Web analytics in real time for deeper insights.

2. SEO Tools:

Ahrefs (https://ahrefs.com/) - SEO tools that are comprehensive for keyword research, backlink analysis, and site audits.

SEMrush (https://www.semrush.com/) - SEO, PPC, and content marketing all in one marketing toolbox.

3. Email Marketing:

Mailchimp (https://mailchimp.com/) - Create and manage email campaigns using simple tools.

ConvertKit (https://convertkit.com/) - Automated email marketing for creators.

4. Content Creation:

Canva (https://www.canva.com/) - Make visually appealing marketing materials.

Grammarly (https://www.grammarly.com/) - Grammar and style tips can help you improve your work.

5. Affiliate Networks:

Amazon Associates (https://affiliate-program.amazon.com/) - Join the biggest affiliate marketing network in the world.

ShareASale (https://www.shareasale.com/) - Contact a wide choice of merchants and products.

6. Podcast

Smart Passive Income Podcast (https://www.smartpassiveincome.com/shows/spi) - Pat Flynn's podcast discusses a variety of topics related to internet commerce, including affiliate marketing.

Remember that these materials and tools are meant to supplement and increase your learning. Make your choices based on your objectives and tastes, and may they help you succeed in the ever-changing world of affiliate marketing. Have fun exploring!

Affiliate Marketing Terminology

Understanding a distinct collection of phrases and vocabulary is required to navigate the world of affiliate marketing. Here's a thorough dictionary to help you understand affiliate marketing jargon:

1. Affiliate: A person or organization who advertises the goods of another business and receives a commission for each sale or lead made via their recommendation.

2. Affiliate Link: An affiliate is issued a unique URL for tracking reasons, which is used to identify and credit the affiliate for purchases or leads.

3. Conversion Rate: The proportion of visitors who do a desired activity, such as making a purchase or completing a form.

4. Cookie: A little amount of data saved on a user's device that assists in tracking their internet behavior, including interactions with affiliate links.

5. CPA (Cost Per Acquisition): The amount paid by an advertiser for each specific activity, such as a sale or lead, produced by the affiliate's marketing efforts.

6. CPC (Cost Per Click): The amount paid by an advertiser for each click on their affiliate link, regardless of whether or not the user makes a purchase.

7. CPL (Cost Per Lead): The fee paid by an advertiser for each qualified lead produced by the affiliate's marketing activities.

8. CTR (Click-Through Rate): The proportion of persons that clicked on an affiliate link vs the total number of people who viewed the link.

9. Deep Linking: Creating an affiliate link that, rather than the homepage, takes people to a particular page on the advertiser's website.

10. EPC (Earnings Per Click): The average amount earned by an affiliate for per click on one of their affiliate links, computed by dividing total earnings by the number of clicks.

11. Merchant: The firm or business that owns the product or service that affiliates are promoting.

12. Niche: A market sector that focuses on a certain kind of product or audience.

13. ROI (Return on Investment): The ratio of net profit to investment cost, commonly represented as a percentage.

14. Sub-Affiliate: An affiliate who is recruited by another affiliate and earns a commission on the recruited affiliate's sales or leads.

15. White Labeling: Rebranding a product or service so that it seems to have been produced by the affiliate, enabling them to market it under their own brand.

This glossary is a brief reference resource to help you understand the terms used in affiliate marketing. Use it to get a better grasp of the industry and communicate more effectively in an ever-changing environment. Happy studying!

Bonus 1: Affiliate Marketing Profitable Niches

The most successful affiliate themes usually fall into one of five general categories: Hobbies, Technology, Finance, Health, and Fashion.

Health and Wellness Industry

A thriving market centered on goods and practices that promote optimum health and well-being. This specialty covers a wide variety of issues, including dietary supplements, mental health services, and exercise programs. With society's increased focus on health and beauty, this area has the potential to be very successful.

Beauty Niche

The emphasis here is on goods and services that try to improve personal appearance and keep a young glow. It may include skincare, cosmetics, and haircare items, as well as anti-aging remedies and beauty tech advancements. As individuals throughout the world emphasize their looks and self-care, the beauty industry continues to flourish. It appeals to people of all genders and ages, and it is always looking for new trends, ideas, and tactics.

Technology and Gaming Niche

Building an affiliate marketing website around a technology specialty, such as software, hardware, or gaming, might lead to great success and consistent organic traffic. This is because technology is always evolving, and consumers want the newest gear.

Finance and Investment Niche

Individuals interested in increasing their wealth and gaining financial independence are catered to in the finance specialty. It is divided into many sub-genres, including bitcoin initiatives, stock market insights, real estate investments, and others. Because a vast populace is continually striving to better their financial situation, the appeal of financial stability and independence makes this area particularly profitable.

High-End Fashion Niche

The high-end fashion niche caters to fashion-forward people who appreciate premium brands and designer items. The high price points of luxury fashion goods and the strong brand loyalty of its buyers drive the profitability of this segment.

Evergreen Affiliate Marketing Niches

While the popularity of certain niches may vary, evergreen niches continually stay lucrative. They revolve around constantly relevant topics.

Fitness and Weight Loss Niche

The fitness and weight loss niche provides items and services that assist customers in reaching their health and fitness objectives, such as home exercise equipment, diet programs, yoga accessories, and other affiliate products pertinent to this market.

Relationship Niche

Advice and tools are provided to assist individuals enhance their relationships. It comprises sub-niches such as the online dating sector, marital counseling services, and parenting advice. The human need for satisfying relationships makes this a wide specialty, yet it has a sizable market.

Gardening Niche

This specialty caters to individuals who want to cultivate plants for beauty or food. This is an excellent affiliate marketing niche for organic gardening, indoor plants, or online landscape design instruction programs. Gardening is a popular pastime for many people, making this an evergreen affiliate marketing vertical.

Pet Niche

You should pay attention to this area as an affiliate marketer since it targets pet owners seeking for items and information to better their dogs' life. What may be classified as a pet niche? A micro specialty, such as training a certain dog breed, cat diet, or aquarium upkeep. People's strong emotional attachment to their pets makes this a lucrative affiliate marketing area.

Online Education Niche

The online education market provides digital learning resources. It might encompass everything from coding lessons to language learning applications to online coaching. This niche stays stable year after year, thanks to the increased desire for flexible learning choices.

Highly Competitive Affiliate Marketing Niches

While competition might be difficult, it also signifies that a market is in strong demand. If you can carve out your own place, they are extremely competitive yet very profitable affiliate categories.

Cooking and Food Niche

Cooking and food is the excellent affiliate niche for people interested in culinary skills, food goods, and diet trends. It may include themes such as vegan recipes and baking supplies.

Tourism and Travel Niche

The tourism and travel specialty caters to customers who are planning holidays or looking for travel assistance. Consider adventurous travel, luxurious lodgings, or travel equipment. However, the urge to travel and experience new locations has oversaturated the niche.

Digital Marketing and SEO Niche

The digital marketing and SEO specialization offers tools to companies looking to increase their online presence. What lies behind this niche? Content marketing, social media strategy specialty websites, and SEO tools.

Online Retail and eCommerce Niche

This specific specialization entails advertising numerous web products. Fashion eCommerce, dropshipping, and home products businesses, as well as tech gadget companies, are examples of sub-niche kinds. Because of the ease of internet buying, this is a highly competitive market.

Lifestyle Niche

There are several niche markets in the lifestyle sector, each catering to a distinct population or lifestyle preference. The breadth of issues in this sector, ranging from minimalist living and luxury lifestyles to sustainable living practices, makes it a very competitive field.

Characteristics of a Profitable Affiliate Marketing Niche

A successful affiliate niche will usually have a:

• a consistent audience

• in great demand

• a plethora of products to promote

• and enough space to provide value with original material.

Choosing the correct niche, on the other hand, is dependent on your interests and skills.

Bonus 2: Copywriting ChatGPT Prompts for Affiliate Marketers

Here are some ChatGPT copywriting prompts for affiliate marketers:

1. Product Description:

"Create an enticing product description for a fitness tracker, emphasizing its features and advantages."

2. Email Subject Line:

"Make a catchy subject line for an email marketing a limited-time discount on a beauty product."

3. Social Media Caption:

"Create an enticing Instagram caption for a new tech device that will entice followers to visit the link and learn more."

4. Call-to-Action (CTA):

"Create a compelling call-to-action for a blog article that encourages visitors to browse a selection of fashion goods via an affiliate link."

5. Banner Ad Copy:

"Create succinct and compelling language for a banner ad offering a kitchen equipment flash sale."

6. Affiliate Program Announcement:

"Create a welcoming and informative announcement for an affiliate program, urging partners to participate and emphasizing the advantages."

7. Product Comparison Introduction:

"Create an interesting start for a blog article comparing two popular computers, stressing their distinct selling qualities."

8. Testimonial Request Email:

"Create an email asking for a testimonial from a happy customer who bought a product via your affiliate link."

9. Affiliate Newsletter Opening:

"Create an interesting beginning paragraph for an affiliate marketing email that introduces the most recent trends and items in the area."

10. Ad Copy for Social Media Ads:

"Create eye-catching ad language for a Facebook ad marketing a travel-related product with an emphasis on adventure and wanderlust."

11. Holiday Promotion Announcement:

"Create a festive statement for a holiday campaign, inviting your audience to take advantage of unique discounts via your affiliate links."

12. Review Article Opening:

"Create excitement and encourage readers to investigate a new smartphone's unique characteristics by writing a great start for a review article."

Feel free to modify these prompts to meet your unique requirements or sector. They may be used to generate innovative and effective text for a variety of marketing products.

Bonus 3: Keywords Research ChatGPT Prompts for Affiliate Marketers

Here are some keyword research suggestions customized to affiliate marketers:

1. Product-Centric Keywords:

"Make a list of product-related keywords for a smartwatch affiliate site."

2. Comparison Keywords:

"Provide keywords for a blog article comparing the most recent DSLR cameras, with an emphasis on features and performance."

3. Best-of Lists Keywords:

"Create keywords for a post emphasizing the 'Top 10 Best Fitness Apps' that would be appropriate for an affiliate pushing health and wellness items."

4. Problem-Solution Keywords:

"Create keywords for a blog article that addresses common skin concerns and suggests skincare items as treatments."

5. Seasonal Keywords:

"Provide seasonal keywords for a holiday-themed affiliate marketing campaign advertising gift ideas in the tech area."

6. Tutorial Keywords:

"Create keywords for a lesson on how to install and use a certain software package, with an emphasis on affiliate marketing."

7. Review Keywords:

"Create keywords for a noise-cancelling headphones product review post that focuses on user experiences and performance."

8. Brand-Specific Keywords:

"Provide keywords for an affiliate marketer pushing products from a certain fashion brand."

9. Long-Tail Keywords:

"Create long-tail keywords for an affiliate site selling eco-friendly home goods."

10. Localized Keywords:

"Create keywords for a regional affiliate marketing campaign offering outdoor equipment and aimed at a certain city or area."

11. Affiliate Program Keywords:

"Provide keywords for material designed to entice affiliate marketers to join a certain affiliate program."

12. Problem-Aware Keywords:

"Create keywords that address typical problems associated with work-from-home setups and propose affiliate products as solutions."

Remember to start with these prompts and then modify the produced keywords to your unique niche and audience. Additionally, for best SEO performance, try employing keyword research tools to confirm and improve your selected phrases.

Request for a Review

Dear Valued Reader,

I hope you enjoy **"A Crash Course in Affiliate Marketing: A Comprehensive Beginner's Guide to Building Massive Passive Income by Leveraging the Most Lucrative Niches"** and find the information both useful and informative. Your input is vital to me, and I would be grateful if you could share your ideas by posting a review.

Your review not only aids in the discovery of the book by other aspiring affiliate marketers, but it also gives vital insights into your own experience. If you feel the book merits five stars, your recommendation may have a big influence.

Please visit https://amazon.com and share your opinions to post a review. Your candid opinion will help shape the future of this book and guide others on their affiliate marketing journey.

Furthermore, I invite you to contact me if you have any questions, recommendations, or difficulties while exploring the affiliate marketing topics in the book. Your success and comprehension are my top concerns, and I'm here to help.

Please feel free to contact me personally at williamquick92@gmail.com I'm here to assist if you have a question regarding a particular idea or need clarity on an approach.

Thank you for taking the time to read this and consider expressing your opinions. Your help meant everything to me.

Best Regards,

William R. Quick

williamquick92@gmail.com,

www.ingramcontent.com/pod-product-compliance
Lightning Source LLC
Chambersburg PA
CBHW082210290526
45794CB00009B/3488